"Thomas Bremer's *Cross and Kremlin* is a sympathetic yet critical interpretation of Russian Orthodoxy by a non-Orthodox expert who loves and understands its varied historical and thematic manifestations. This book will be welcomed by specialists and nonexperts alike."

— Paul Mojzes
Rosemont College

"The history of Russia and the history of the Russian Orthodox Church are inherently connected. Written by a seasoned scholar, this highly readable, chronological, succinct yet thorough explanation of the thousand-year history of the Orthodox Church in Russia will become essential reading for scholars and students interested in Russian Orthodoxy, Eastern Christianity, and Russian history."

— Ines Angeli Murzaku
Seton Hall University

D1598444

CROSS AND KREMLIN

A Brief History of the
Orthodox Church in Russia

Thomas Bremer

Translated by

Eric W. Gritsch

William B. Eerdmans Publishing Company
Grand Rapids, Michigan / Cambridge, U.K.

Originally published 2007 in German as
Kreuz und Kreml: Kleine Geschichte der orthodoxen Kirche in Russland
© 2007 Verlag Herder, Freiburg im Breisgau

English translation © 2013 Wm. B. Eerdmans Publishing Co.

Published 2013 by Wm. B. Eerdmans Publishing Co.
2140 Oak Industrial Drive N.E., Grand Rapids, Michigan 49505 /
P.O. Box 163, Cambridge CB3 9PU U.K.

Printed in the United States of America

19 18 17 16 15 14 13   7 6 5 4 3 2 1

Library of Congress Cataloging-in-Publication Data

Bremer, Thomas, 1957-
[Kreuz und Kreml. English]
Cross and Kremlin: a brief history of the Orthodox Church in Russia /
Thomas Bremer; translated by Eric W. Gritsch.
pages   cm
Includes bibliographical references and index.
ISBN 978-0-8028-6962-3 (pbk.: alk. paper)
1. Orthodox Eastern Church — Russia (Federation) — History.
2. Russia (Federation) — Church history.   I. Title.

BX485.B7413   2013
281.9′47 — dc23

2013010381

www.eerdmans.com

Contents

Contents

Preface to the English Edition

⁓

T his book is written by an author who is neither Russian nor Orthodox. However, a certain distance can sometimes facilitate greater
comprehension of a subject. I tried to describe the Russian Orthodox
Church in its history and in its current shape, on the basis of research
that makes it more interesting for a reader who is not a specialist. That is
why the book is not written in a chronological order. The first chapter offers a survey of the historical development of Russian Orthodoxy from
the beginnings until today. In the subsequent chapters, the most important areas of ecclesiastical life are analyzed, but always from a historical
perspective. The current shape of the Orthodox Church in Russia can be
understood only with regard to its development through the centuries
and with regard to its attitudes toward phenomena such as the state, "the
West," and the Greek-Byzantine world.

The book was written for a German audience. Sometimes, parallels
are drawn to the German situation, or a German aspect of a phenomenon
will be especially emphasized. I tried to reduce such examples in the
translation, and I also updated statistics for the period after 2007, when
the book was written.

It is with great pleasure that I thank all persons who were involved in
the English edition. Above all, I want to thank the translator, the late
Eric W. Gritsch, for his enormous efforts and skills in bringing my German text into fine English; he passed away unexpectedly after he had
translated this book. I also want to express my gratitude to Dr. Norman A. Hjelm, who initiated and pursued efforts to publish the work in
English. Finally, I owe a debt of gratitude to William B. Eerdmans Jr., the

president of Wm. B. Eerdmans Publishing Company, for his readiness to publish the book in English. And I want to extend a warm thank you to my friend and colleague Professor Alfred Sproede, who read the proofs of the English text and gave me many useful hints.

Summer 2012   THOMAS BREMER

Introduction

The perception of Russia and, above all, its Christianity is frequently marked by prejudices in the West. Images of a "holy Russia," or of a "Russian soul," allegedly marked by a special ability to suffer, but also by the wideness of the Russian landscape, or a special interest in icons and in features of Russian spirituality often characterize the way Russia and its church are seen. But such a sentimental approach fails to recognize important elements and developments of Russian church history that are of central meaning for an understanding of Russia and its Christianity.

In this connection, a significant aspect is the important question of Russia's affiliation with "Europe." A contrast is constructed by the widely spread superficial view that identifies Europe with the European Union. But the contrast lacks historical evidence. The problem also appears occasionally in assumptions about the ability of Orthodoxy to be European. The process of integration that made members of the Russian Orthodox Church (in the Baltic states) citizens of the European Union, together with other members of Orthodox churches (for example, in the Balkan states and, above all, in Greece and Cyprus, but also in Bulgaria and Romania), contributes to the fact that representatives of the Russian Orthodox Church comment ever more frequently on European themes, especially those that deal with the spiritual foundations of the continent. That is why the question of the geographical, political, historical, cultural, and religious affiliation of Russia with Europe must again be considered.

This is not at all a new question for Russian Orthodoxy. History shows that the affiliation with the West has always been a central theme for Russia and Russian Orthodoxy. Its geographical location forced Russia to develop special relationships with Asia, and its affiliation with two continents has played a significant role in its intellectual history since the nineteenth century. But Russia also perceived itself as a European nation, and the remaining European nations — that meant the West for Russia — always made contacts with Russia, be they economic, political, warlike, or intellectual. Nevertheless, mutual ignorance is still widespread today.

This book attempts to remedy this fault by exposing, on the one hand, the peculiarity and, in many respects, the singularity of Russian Christianity, and on the other hand, its affiliation with Europe. The book also should provide an insight into the past and present of the Russian Orthodox Church even though it is not more than a first guide, given its limited size. It also is not simply a chronological narrative of Russian church history, from its origins to the present. After introducing the most significant epochs, developments, and events, the volume presents central themes and problems in their historical sequence, with an eye on their historical significance and, whenever possible, also always with special attention to the situation today. Accordingly, various issues are elaborated, such as monasticism, theology, and relations with the West. Treatment of such issues cannot be exhaustive but must remain limited to focal points. That is why some aspects are also repeatedly mentioned. Moreover, there is no detailed bibliography; footnotes identify the sources of quotations and refer to some significant secondary literature in German and to a few works in English. The result is a survey of the most important themes of Russian church history. It may suffice to be a satisfactory introduction.

I am grateful to my coworkers Stephanie van de Loo, Maria Wernsmann, Michael Altmeier, Alfons Brüning (now Nijmegen), and Christoph Mühl. They read the manuscript and offered valuable advice. I am indebted to Friedemann Kluge for a significant suggestion. Heike Dörrenbächer frequently helped me with a good word and wise counsel, not only during the time of working on this book, and my conversations with Stefanie Schiffer and our going to church together became very important for me. I thank both of them very much for their friendship and support!

Münster, June 2007   THOMAS BREMER

Practical Pointers

Russian names and words are not transliterated after one of the scientific transliteration systems, but rather according to the BGN/PCGN romanization standard that makes such names and words easily readable for non-Russian speakers. Some names are written in their English form (Alexander, not Aleksandr).

Today, Russian Orthodoxy designates itself as "Russian Orthodox Church" (ROC), a designation of modern origin. Prior to 1917, the designations "Russian Orthodoxy" and simply "Russian Church" are used.

Bishops and other monks are identified only by their first names (their monastic names) according to Orthodox custom. The family name of persons of modern times is added in parentheses in each chapter when the person is introduced.

CHAPTER ONE

Demarcations

Subject Matter

Russian church history could be written in several ways. (1) One could do it in regard to the Russians as a nation, a "folk." This would be a history of Christianity among Russians in which Orthodoxy certainly played a key role. But other Christian and indeed also non-Christian views and communities among Russians would have to be considered. No special attention would be given to national borders and orders, even though one would have to ponder the question how long Russians have been known as a nation and how one defines a nation. (2) One could view the task as a history of the Russian Orthodox Church (ROC), which today is the largest religious community among Russians. Consequently, other important churches would have to be excluded, such as Protestants, Catholics, and indeed in a certain sense also the Old Believers who split from Russian Orthodoxy in the seventeenth century. But, above all, the topic would then not be limited to Russia because Russian Orthodoxy also exists in other countries. Moreover, one would have to take into account how long the ROC existed and deal with its predecessors. (3) One could focus not on the nation but on the state, that is, Russia. This would be a history of the church, other churches, or even religion in Russia, that is, the territory of the Russian Federation today and its predecessors, the Soviet Union, the Russian Empire, etc. The Roman Catholic Church and various Protestant churches would be included. It would even make sense to deal with the history of non-Christian religions, such as Judaism, Islam, and Buddhism. All of them are of great importance for Russia.

1

A definition of the content of the topic becomes problematic. For in the course of history not only the borders of the various forms of government changed, understanding themselves as exclusively or predominantly "Russian," but also the ecclesiastical forms, their juridical affiliation, and the geographical space where they dominated. Russian church history would be a little like a German church history in which locations like Salzburg, Utrecht, Prague, Vienna, and Breslau played an important role even though they do not belong to Germany today. Moreover, the juridical forms of the Roman Catholic Church in Germany today, such as the German Bishops' Conference, had differently organized predecessors. That is why it will be necessary, in the course of the historical narrative, to include territorial variations that imply also variations of the subject matter.

This church history focuses on the Orthodox Church among Eastern Slavs, respectively, Russians. Accordingly, it is not the story of the phenomenon "Christianity" or "religion" among ethnic Russians or in Russia, but the history of Eastern Orthodox Christendom. Since Russian Christianity began among Eastern Slavs, who in the tenth century were located in modern-day Ukraine, above all in Kiev, the historical description must reach beyond today's Russian territory. The shift of focus to the north occurred later when Moscow, then St. Petersburg, and finally again Moscow became the capital in the twentieth century. Russian church history, therefore, begins in Kiev. The occasional political tensions between Russia and Ukraine can be understood in the light of this background. Some Russians have a hard time accepting that Kiev, "the mother of the Russian cities" and the cradle of Russian Orthodoxy, is today in a foreign country. Conversely, many Ukrainians find it hard to recognize the baptism of Russia in the old Kiev. These issues must also be considered.

A "Greek" church was the first ecclesiastical organization in Russia in the tenth century, with a metropolitan as its head, chosen, or at least confirmed, by the patriarch of Constantinople. The last of these metropolitans in the fifteenth century was still a Greek, not a Slav. The Russian Church became independent only after him; that is, it could choose its head and did not need confirmation from anybody. In subsequent centuries the church was led by metropolitans, by patriarchs, and by a governing body called "the Most Holy Governing Synod." Finally, today, after the effects of the twentieth century, a patriarch is once again the head of the church. The form of the ecclesiastical organization also changed in various ways. Accordingly, these changing forms of one and the same church on a changing territory must also be considered.

At the time of the Christianization of the "Rus'" (the name for the Kiev state), that is, in the tenth century, there was no national consciousness. The individual tribes of the Eastern Slavs had obscure names. But they all had a common language, namely, old Slavonic or Old Church Slavonic. In modern times, these tribes became the three large East Slavic nationalities of Russians, Ukrainians, and Belarusians. Today they live, for the most part, in countries named after them (or they are named after the countries); there may still be fluid borders among them, and double identities occur. Insofar as the Russian Church has expanded, or still expands, its jurisdiction to Ukrainians and Belarusians, attention must also be paid to these peoples.

Many aspects, therefore, need to be sorted out as they relate to the development of Russian church history because it also and always evolved in contact with other churches, just as the various Russian countries interrelated with other countries or national formations. These dynamics between territory, nation, and ecclesiastical organization must always be noted and elucidated.

Regarding methodology: a "brief history" suggests that there is a chronological sequence. But it should not be in the foreground. The next chapter surveys the most important epochs and events. But then subsequent chapters focus on basic themes: Christianization and expansion, ecclesiastical structures, church and state, theology and religious thought, monasticism, spirituality and religiosity, Russian Orthodoxy and the West, as well as dissidence. It is, therefore, more important to present these phenomena and their peculiarities in their historical development and contemporary situation than to convey simply the sequence of events and phenomena. The second chapter, therefore, is designed to make the important epochs known as presuppositions for the treatment of the above-mentioned themes. Here, of course, some aspects will become focal points.

Territory

Today, the Russian Federation *(Rossiyskaya Federatsiya)*[1] is the largest country in the world. Its area is about 6.6 million square miles — 11.5 per-

---

1. The Russian language employs two different words as adjectives for "Russian": (1) *russkiy,* referring to persons, language, culture, etc., and (2) *rossiyskiy,* relating to the Russian state — the adjective "Russian," as attached to the noun "Federation."

cent of the surface of the earth. Germany comprises about 140,000 square miles and would fit mathematically about fifty times into the territory of Russia. The territory has an east-west extension of about 5,580 miles, from the Baltic Sea to the Sea of Japan. The largest north-south extension amounts to 2,480 miles. A trip around Russia, along its borders and coastlines, would consist of 37,820 miles.

Today, Russia has about 145 million inhabitants, almost three-quarters of them (74 percent) in cities and only a smaller part in the country. There are fifteen cities with a million or more residents. Moscow has 10 million; St. Petersburg has about 4 million. As the name of the country puts it, Russia is federatively constructed. There are altogether eighty-nine different parts of the Federation: twenty-one republics, six regions, forty-nine provinces, and two capitals (traditionally, Moscow and St. Petersburg are so designated) with a special status, in addition to ten "Autonomous Districts" and one "Autonomous Territory." The decision of President Putin in 2000 to divide the country into eight huge regions (federation districts) where he himself could appoint "plenipotentiary representatives," strengthens the centralizing component of the federative structure. The largest nation in the Russian Federation is the Russians, who constitute 89 percent of the entire population; 2.35 percent are Ukrainians; various other nations live in the Federation, in part concentrated in specific regions, but in part dispersed all over the country.

There were fifteen Soviet republics in the Soviet Union, which fell apart at the end of 1991. The Russian Republic (Russian Socialist Federative Soviet Republic, or RSFSR) was the largest. It occupied 76 percent of the space of the entire USSR and is the direct predecessor of today's Russia. This enormous size characterizes the country. History is always bound to a concrete space or to concrete spaces. A country with such a scope must necessarily develop differently than a smaller one. The development is affected by very practical matters, such as various time zones (the time difference between Moscow and Vladivostok is two hours greater than that between Germany and New York; so one views Moscow's 9:00 P.M. news at 4:00 A.M. the next day in the East) and climate zones, and practical problems connected with them, such as transportation. Vast areas in Siberia are still not opened up, and when rivers are not iced over, airplanes and helicopters are the only means of transportation to places not reached by the Siberian railroad. A glance at a map of Siberia clearly shows that there is hardly a road for hundreds of miles. These circumstances caused radical differences between cities in the European part and cities in the other parts of Russia. Although the attempt of the Soviet system failed to eliminate these differences through an accelerated modernization, one can, however, see very different developments, or stages of modernization, side by side, in one particular place.

In recent years, the designation "territory" has played a significant role in ecumenical relations because the ROC claims a "canonical territory" for itself. In this region it is the dominant church with exclusive rights to evangelize. "Territory" basically means a self-contained region with clear borders. It appeared in history only very recently, and only where there are solid natural borders, such as coasts or rivers. Without such natural boundaries the borders of sovereign regions are not stable and change often. In the first phases of Russian church history, one cannot speak of a stable territory. The structures in question were not states in the modern sense but forms of dominion closely tied to a specific ruler. Military campaigns subjugated other tribes, and they became tributaries. But such "territories" were by no means clearly defined or safe. Dependence had not necessarily other consequences than being a taxable tributary. Moreover, it is also significant for Russian church history that there was a vast and unexplored space in the east that did not "belong" to anyone, namely, Siberia. Arguments about borders arose, above all, in the west, facing Poland, Lithuania, and Sweden, in part also in the south, facing Turkey, but not in the north where there was no political power until one reached the Arctic Ocean. So there was no resistance to a Russian claim for this space, and hardly any in the east, which was for Russia, like the west was for the United States, an unowned, uncivilized, and unassigned vast space.

Since the early modern period, one can speak of firm Russian borders (which, however, frequently changed through war and peace). But the question of ecclesiastical territory is quite different. Believers, who until this time belonged to Russian Orthodoxy, fell into the realm of other Orthodox church structures, or regions, removed from Russian ecclesiastical jurisdiction. Thus, the territory of the ROC was no longer identical with the territory where its members lived. Within these processes there arose a consciousness of a "proper" affiliation of this Orthodox population with the ROC. It found its clearest expression in the modern way of speaking of the canonical territory. The ROC established the solid borders of this territory for the first time in 2000. It was the region of the former USSR, but without Georgia and Armenia (where there are Orthodox churches, even though the Armenian Church, as an Oriental-Orthodox, that is, "Old Oriental" Church, is not in communion with the ROC). This commitment to a canonical territory and the reasoning behind it had great consequences for ecumenical relations. But the space where Orthodox believers of the Russian Church live and the territory claimed by it are not always identical. This situation caused a series of problems that are still not satisfactorily resolved today.

CHAPTER TWO

Epochs

A Russian church history consisting of epochs can be guided, at least for the early period, by the spaces where it occurred. For the time of Christianization, it was Kiev, the empire of Kiev or the Kievan Rus'. This informal association of East Slavic tribes, which was no state in a modern sense, moved to the north after the turn of the millennium in connection with the attacks of Asian tribes (Mongols and Tartars). There was not yet a clear and enduring main location. For the time being, the city of Vladimir (northeast of Moscow) was the residence of the grand prince, then Moscow. The Moscow empire grew and became one of the most important political factors in eastern Europe. It always had a double relationship with the rest of Europe: a consciousness of affiliation and solidarity with the west of the continent, expressed at specific periods in dynastic relations, and also a mutual sentiment of strangeness and of its own special way that was strongly connected with religion. The Orthodox Church was not the only one with the conviction to be the only true church. But this consciousness also led to a particular separation because of spatial isolation. On the one hand, it was difficult to accept influences from the outside quickly and thoroughly, and on the other hand, it created a feeling that the Russians simply did not belong to other European nations as one among many. It will become evident that Russia's relation to the West would have to remain a central theme for Russian history and also for church history.

In the eighteenth century, Tsar Peter the Great tried to break through this isolation by opening up Russia to the West. The most significant sign of this was the creation of a new capital, named after the tsar's patron saint and with a Western name, namely, St. Petersburg ("Sankt Peterburg" in today's Russian). In the eighteenth and nineteenth centuries, the destiny of the church was determined from there, even though no patriarch but a governing body, a so-called synod, led the church. In connection with the October Revolution of 1917, the patriarchal office was again introduced, and Moscow became the seat of church leadership as well as the nation's capital, which it remains today. One can, therefore, construct a rough pattern of epochs in the light of the cities from where the Rus', or later, Russia, was led: Kiev, Vladimir, Moscow, St. Petersburg, Moscow. These periods and the central events of Russian church history constitute the criteria for structuring the survey of the historical development of Russian Orthodoxy.

Christianization

The northwestern region of today's Ukraine counts as the original home of the Slavs who spread to central, eastern, and southwestern Europe in the mass migration known as *Völkerwanderung.* Place-names show that their early areas of settlement were larger than where they are settled today. The East Slavs, in part, remained in the area of Ukraine, an area around the river Dnepr, and, in part, settled in Finnish and Baltic areas. The nations of Russians, Ukrainians, and Belarusians were to develop from them. In the ninth and tenth centuries there were not yet different national formations; the East Slavs were subdivided into tribes. The area of the settlement, as well as its inhabitants, was called Rus'. The origin of the name was unclear for a long time and is still debated. But it is probably connected with the Finnish *ruotsi,* "rower" (the word still means in Finnish "Sweden" today). There was a connection between Scandinavia and the East Slavs. Recent investigations furnish evidence for a genetic mark, shared by Scandinavians and Slavs but missing in all other Europeans. Even though the value of such findings is debated, they still reveal historical connections. They appear after the year 700 when non-Christian Normans, so-called Varangians, demanded tributes from Slavs in the northeast of today's Russia. Later, they advanced farther south, always along rivers, in order to find a way across the Dnepr "from the *Varangians* to the Greeks,"[1] as it is said in a chronicle.

1. "The Rus' Primary Chronicle," for example, in the edition by Samuel Hazzard Cross and Olgerd P. Sherbowitz-Wetzor (Cambridge, Mass.: Mediaeval Academy of America, 1953).

About the end of the ninth century, a center originated in Kiev, named Rus'. For some time at least the upper classes were still "Varangian," clearly evident in proper names in the sources. This Kievan Rus' campaigned several times against Constantinople. In the course of the tenth century, the existence of Christianity and of church buildings is repeatedly mentioned. But an effective and lasting Christianization began only in 988 when Prince Vladimir ("the saint") agreed to be baptized and ordered his subjects to accept Christianity. In the background were quarrels about the political power of Constantinople and their solutions through a dynastic connection between the imperial family and the Kiev prince; the connection was made possible only by his baptism. Thus it was also a question of Christianization "from above." Later, this event was often called "the baptism of the Rus'." The act of a joint baptism of all inhabitants of Kiev in the river Dnepr by order of the prince (not historically demonstrable) has become a significant motif of Russian historiography.

The Russian Church was founded from Constantinople. The first bishops and priests came from the imperial city, and for many centuries the Rus' remained canonically dependent on Constantinople. Metropolitans were appointed there; frequently, they were also Greeks who did not understand the Slavonic language and had to learn it. Kiev was dependent on the patriarch in Constantinople and, in turn, dioceses were subordinated to Kiev. The transmission of the faith from Constantinople was the reason that Russia received Christianity in its eastern, Greek, form, not in the western, Latin, one. At the time of the "baptism of the Rus'," the schism between Rome and Constantinople had not yet occurred. But there were clearly defined juridical areas between East and West. The two traditions approved each other but they were different in a number of ways. One was the use of the vernacular common in the East. Texts were translated from the Greek into Old Slavonic. Consequently, an independent ecclesiastical literature emerged very early in the vernacular.

The Kievan Rus'

The new faith spread very quickly through a Christianization "from above." But the phenomenon of the *dvoyeveriye* (Russian for "double faith") remained alive for a long time, the transmission of individual elements (above all in the realm of popular piety) from the customary religion to the new faith. On the other hand, the transmission certainly generated opposition from the representatives of the new, now official religion, but they could not prevent the long endurance of the *dvoyeveriye.*

Besides Kiev, the remaining cities of the East Slavic area were also Christianized and received bishops who were not Greeks, as was customary, but ethnic Slavs. These cities were ruled in different ways. Especially Novgorod must be mentioned here because with its "council" (*veche* in Russian), after 1136 it did not develop a monarchic form of government but developed one that even contained early democratic (or rather, oligarchic) elements. The cities were the main locations of the respective tribes and were usually ruled by princes; the position of grand prince was reserved for the city of Kiev. Since the position of grand prince was not to be bequeathed to a son but to the first younger brother, warlike quarrels ensued between uncles and nephews as well as between brothers when both claimed this honor.

The rule of Grand Prince Yaroslav ("the Wise") in the eleventh century can be called the flowering period of the Kievan Rus'. This relates not only to political power, the expansion, but also to the cultural achievements of the political system.

Monasticism became very quickly significant within the church. Yaroslav himself founded many monasteries. The Kiev Cave Monastery became a center of monastic life in the Rus'. Very soon, numerous other monasteries originated. They produced the most significant documents of the Old Russian literature, most famous of which is the "Primary Chronicle" or "Tale of Bygone Years," earlier called Nestor's Chronicle of the year 1113, named after its alleged author. The codification of the language was the presupposition for the origin of an ecclesiastical literature that, besides liturgical texts and chronicles, very soon also included lives of saints, sermons, and the so-called *Pateriki,* that is, "books of fathers," biographies of monks in a monastery. In addition, there also were translations of Greek authors and some other kinds of writings. There has been a detailed discussion whether these sources were received from the Byzantine tradition or represent new creations. During the Soviet period, Russian scholars attached great importance to the fact that an independent literature evolved already early in the Rus'.

There also was a quest for creative independence in ecclesiastical architecture in the Kievan Rus'. Although influenced by Byzantium, it still developed its own style. The Sophia Church in Kiev is an impressive testimony to the early building activity. Noteworthy is the development of building cupolas, which are characteristic of Russian churches still today. First, the churches were built in the Byzantine cross-cupola style; the number of columns and support pillars could be reduced to six, and in the twelfth century finally to four. This became characteristic for Russian churches.

Toward the end of the twelfth century, the Rus' disintegrated. But the name survived for some time and referred to various territories. In 1169, Kiev was conquered by Grand Prince Andrey; so there was no longer a regular succession to the throne. Now, the conqueror of the city claimed the title of Kiev Grand Prince but remained in his capital Vladimir, northeast of Moscow. A period followed when divided principalities acquired a greater independence from the grand prince. Three centers emerged. One principality was in the southwest, with Galich (Halich) the most important location; here, one can observe an orientation toward the West, also quite obvious geographically. In the northwest, Novgorod, boasting its autonomy, became more and more important; and in the northeast it was Vladimir, with Moscow, first mentioned in 1147, ascending slowly to ever greater significance. These divided principalities were no longer tied to tribes but were tied to the areas around main locations.

The center of power moved to the north only gradually. It had already been intimated by Grand Prince Andrey, or, more precisely: the center of power in the northeast prevailed (with the later inclusion of Novgorod) while the one in the southwest came to Lithuania and Poland and left the federation of principalities. This development also affected the church. The metropolitan stayed for a while in Kiev. But in 1299, after the destruction of his capital by the Tartars, he, too, transferred to Vladimir and kept the title Metropolitan of Kiev. In Kiev, a new metropolitanate was now founded. In the course of time, and after dissolutions and new foundations, it was increasingly influenced by the West, that is, by Poland and Lithuania. The question of the legitimacy of this foundation, of its continuity, and of the "true" church of Kiev is, in the final analysis, still today a reason for differences of opinions in the ecclesiastical sphere between Moscow and Ukraine.

The Rus' clearly differed in many respects from the Western Middle Ages. That is why the term "Middle Ages" cannot readily be applied to it. The aforementioned periodization shows how very different the Russian development is from the west-European one. The relationships between the rulers and the nobility developed differently, and the lack of a feudal economy (in the sense of a legally structured, corporate society) caused many developments in Russia to be very different from the West: the commitment to the employer and to a specific territory, to estates, to chivalry, and, finally, to a middle class. There was even talk about the lack of a society in Russia until the nineteenth century.

The development in the divided principalities of the Rus' was shaped, above all, in the thirteenth century by developments in foreign policy east and west of the Rus', namely, the conquests by Asian tribes, Tartars and Mongols, as well as by attempted conquests on the part of Swedes and the Teutonic Order. Whether there is a connection between the two is questionable. But it plays a significant role in the Russian perception.

After 1223, tribes from the Asian steppe threatened the Rus'. By the middle of the century, they had conquered all significant cities, except Novgorod. They were to rule over the Rus' for more than a century. To-day, this period is called "the yoke of the Tartars," even though the de-pendency was limited, above all, to the duty of paying tribute and of ren-dering occasional military service. The new rulers established their capital, Sarai (where the Volga River flows into the Caspian Sea), at the edge of the Russian territory. There, they welcomed envoys and received bearers of tributes. If necessary, they staged their campaigns from there as a means to punish or discipline; but their military or administrative presence in Russia was not enduring. Accordingly, the principalities of the Rus' managed, little by little, to throw off this foreign oppression dur-ing the fourteenth century. The battle on the Field of Snipes (at the Don River) in 1380 was instrumental. There, Grand Prince Dmitriy of Moscow (also known as "The One from the Don," *Donskoy*) was able to crush, for the first time, the dominion of the Tartars. Formally, their dominion still remained in the form of paying tribute until 1476.

The church remained largely unaffected by these developments. The Tartars proved to be relatively tolerant of religion, and the Orthodox Church did not have to pay tribute to them. It even established its own bishopric in Sarai. There was no systematic persecution of the church by foreign rulers, and there was little interference in ecclesiastical life. Whether the strengthening of monasticism, with significant new monas-teries in the fourteenth century, can be traced to this situation is unclear. But it is important that affiliation with Orthodoxy created a significant difference from the Tartars, the Swedes, and the Teutonic Knights. It be-came a mark that established identity.

The foreign threat from the west first appeared in the attempt of the Teutonic Order to expand its area of influence to the east and to Christian-

The Kievan Rus'

All names are given in the Russian version, even if they belong today to other states and have other forms

ize the pagan Baltic tribes. The threat to Novgorod by the knights of the order was simultaneous with the invasion of the Tartars. A little later, the Swedes and the Lithuanians marched against the city. In 1240, Prince Alexander of Novgorod defeated the Swedes at the Neva River (thus the added name Nevskiy) and, in 1242, the army of the Teutonic Knights on the frozen Peypus Lake. Thus their advance stopped.

On the one hand, Russian perception judged these attempts to advance as the attempt of Western Christianity to turn the East Slav territory into its area of influence and to make Orthodoxy meaningless there. On the other hand, Russians judged these attempts as a betrayal by their western fellow-Christians because they occurred when the Rus' was threatened from the Asian steppe. Instead of hurrying to help their endangered fellow believers, the "Latins" tried to gain a strategic advantage from the weakness of the Russian principalities. Thus the victories of Alexander Nevskiy were not only of military significance but also of great symbolic significance, and the figure of the canonized prince was always called to mind when Russia was threatened by incursions from the west, including the ones during World War II. The advance of Roman Catholicism and the claims of the papacy were stopped by the military successes, and so Orthodoxy remained also the prevailing faith west of the Rus'.

The decision of Lithuania in 1385 to accept Christianity in its Western form indicated a turn to the Catholic world, above all, to Poland. All later mutual contacts and the loss of Kiev to Lithuania made the ancient principality insignificant for Russian history. It shared the fate of the principalities ruled by Lithuania after they had belonged to the Kievan Rus'. But in this connection, a basic decision of Alexander Nevskiy was important, namely, to leave Novgorod in the federation with the remaining principalities and not ally itself with the Teutonic Order against the Tartars. Novgorod had a tradition of concentrating its trade on western Europe and was relatively independent. The decision preserved the unity of the remaining Slavic principalities.

From the Rus' to the Moscow Empire

It is not quite clear why Moscow evolved from small beginnings to become the center of the empire; there are no convincing "necessary" reasons for it, at any rate. The totally insignificant provincial city did amass wealth, and its rise was certainly made possible by its location at the intersection of water and land routes. The Moscow princes succeeded in incorporating individual divided principalities into their realm and permanently attaining the office of a grand prince in 1328. In the same year, the metropolitan, who had already lived for some years in Moscow, moved his official residence there from Vladimir. But he still called himself "metropolitan of Kiev." The grand princes of Moscow became wealthy through the Tartar politics of tributes and through their own skills. Favorable conditions prevented any threats from other princes. The defeat of the Tartars by Dmitriy Donskoy also helped to strengthen the city. Despite dynastic quarrels and problems, the prominent opposition of Moscow within the principalities could not be questioned after the early fourteenth century.

Yet, the Russian Church was still under the jurisdiction of Constantinople, and the confirmation, or nomination, of the metropolitan had to come from the imperial city. Moreover, he bore the title Metropolitan of Kiev and of All the Rus', which, of course, no longer corresponded to reality. In the fifteenth century Kiev was Lithuanian, and its local rulers had made repeated efforts to install their own metropolitan.

Global historical developments ensured that the Russian Church became independent of Constantinople. The increasing threat to the capital of the Byzantine Empire by the Ottomans led to a desire for ecclesiastical unity with Rome in order to gain military support from the western European countries. After long negotiations, a union was concluded in 1439 at the Council of Ferrara-Florence. The ecclesiastical unity between East and West was to be restored. The union was supported, above all, by the Byzantine emperor, who was present at the negotiations, as well as by the patriarch of Constantinople (who died during the council). Moreover, almost all the attending bishops gave their consent. Resistance against the union arose among the population of Constantinople. Attempts were made to have it accepted, but the military support from the West never materialized. Ottomans conquered the city in 1453 and brought an end to the Byzantine Empire after more than a thousand years. The emperor was killed during the defense of the city. There was no longer an "Orthodox" empire. Although friends as well as enemies of the union sat on the patriarchal throne in the years between union agreement and the conquest of the city, the new rulers accepted only patriarchs who were unfavorably disposed toward Rome.

Still, in 1431, the patriarch had rejected a candidate as metropolitan of Kiev because he had been very much favored in Moscow to be the head of the church. Instead, he nominated a Greek, Isidore, who was a friend of the union since its inception. After the end of the council, Isidore traveled to Moscow to proclaim the ecclesiastical union there. But he found no sympathy in Moscow, which harbored reservations against such an enterprise and no sympathy for concessions being made to the Latins. When Isidore mentioned the name of the pope during the liturgy, it aroused so much resentment that he was arrested. He was able to escape, went to Rome, and died in 1463 as a cardinal of the Roman Church.

Russian Orthodoxy now had no leader and also could not rely on Constantinople to supply one because the patriarch was, of course, also a friend of the union. So the grand prince decided in 1448 to choose a bishop as metropolitan who had been rejected earlier by the patriarch, Iona of Ryazan. This meant, in fact, that the Russian Church was now independent; it determined who should be its head, and it was not dependent on any patriarch. It, therefore, was autocephalous. When Constantinople fell five years later, it was only a matter of form when a synod decided in 1459 on autocephaly. Two years later, the title of the ecclesiastical head was adjusted to existing realities by omitting the words "of Kiev." The title now was Metropolitan of Moscow and of All the Rus'.

The position of Moscow became stronger again, and served as the foundation for a special self-understanding of Moscow, of Russia, and above all, of Russian Orthodoxy. This was illustrated later when the grand prince became emperor (tsar) and the metropolitan became a patriarch. There also developed a special consciousness of history within Russian Orthodoxy, an awareness of being destined to play a role in the history of salvation; Russia and its church were to be the last free Orthodox bastion. As a result, the Russia of Moscow became, in some respect, the legacy of Byzantium. To it belonged, for example, the adoption of some elements of the Byzantine court protocol, but also the marriage of Grand Prince Ivan III to a niece of the last Byzantine ruler. The idea of Moscow as a third Rome, which was supposed to be linked to a special sense of mission, originated at this time and also fit this context. But it played no special role and has been excessively interpreted.[2]

An empire under the undisputed rule of Moscow arose from the former federation of principalities. In a process known later as the "gathering of the Russian lands," all the principalities were incorporated into Mos-

2. At this time, ideas of Russia as the "new Israel" were to emphasize the greatness and significance of the country.

cow. At the end of the fifteenth century, Novgorod, the greatest rival, was moved by force into the federation of states. At the same time, the duty to pay tribute to the Tartars also ended, and the titles "tsar" and "independent ruler" (*samoderzhets*, a translation of the Greek "autocrat") appeared for the first time.

This phase of the Moscow period is characterized by encounters between the old, customary Russian element and new influences and conceptions coming, above all, from the West. Already the rejection of the Union of Florence indicated the isolated situation of the Russian Church. Hardly any exchange with other churches occurred, but rather relationships with them eroded. To be sure, Orthodox people from the various parts of the Ottoman Empire visited Moscow, and, in turn, Russian monks visited Mount Athos. But the few contacts with Western Christians produced no lasting effects. Rather, such encounters usually disclosed a lack of understanding for each other. It is, therefore, not surprising that in the seventeenth century even a liturgical reform based on Greek sources was perceived as an illegitimate innovation, causing the greatest ecclesiastical schism in Russian history, the so-called "schism of the Old Believers." It illustrates a phenomenon that periodically reemerged within Russian history and church history, namely, the opposition between "Russian" and "the new."

The monasteries in Russia played an increasingly larger role. Toward the end of the fifteenth century, a third of the country was monastic property. So monasteries became not only a spiritual factor but also an economic one. This, too, was to generate again and again in history desires of the state. But first, there was a dispute between two groups of monks about monastic poverty. More and more monks could no longer see the ideal of poverty realized in the rich monasteries. They, therefore, preferred hermitage. The monk Nil Sorskiy tried to link the ideal of poverty with communal life by creating associations of hermits who revived some memories about praxis in the early church. His ideological opponent was the monk Joseph of Volokolamsk, who argued that there must be rich monasteries, albeit with strict discipline and obedience to the abbot. In this dispute between the "unselfish" and the "Josephites," made more complicated through the appearance of a heretical group, the disciples of Joseph finally prevailed at the beginning of the sixteenth century, not only to the delight of the emperor, who was also afraid of the rich and mighty monasteries. In Russian church history, one can observe again and again attempts of the state to acquire properties of the church. But for a long time, the church paid a price for the existence of rich monasteries with large properties, namely, the promise of loyalty to the state.

The turn from the sixteenth to the seventeenth century brought the only change of dynasty to Russia. Until 1598, a line could be traced to Ryurik, a Varangian ancestor of the Russian rulers. Now quarrels arose, known as "the time of troubles," with Boris Godunov playing a decisive role. In this epoch, the archenemies from the west, Swedes and, above all, Poles, brought great distress to the Russian Empire. Moscow was besieged several times; the Poles even managed to occupy it for several years. One of the insurrections shortly before the end of the Polish occupation was led by Patriarch Germogen. In times of crisis, the church felt called to accept governmental responsibility. Only in 1613 was the Romanov dynasty, with Tsar Mikhail, chosen to head the country; it stayed in power until 1917. So there were only two dynasties in the millennial history of the monarchy in Russia — an astonishing continuity, making changes of power extremely rare events.

The events in "the time of troubles" are also important for the Russian view of the West. For they were judged, with some justification, as another attempt of the Catholic West to bring Russia under its control by force and tricks. A closer look at these events shows how valid this point of view is. The significance of these events for the national consciousness becomes evident in the fact that in the year 2005, November 4, the day of the Kremlin's liberation from the Poles, was declared Day of National Unity as a substitute for the commemoration day of the October Revolution. In this manner, national memory was focused on an event that stands for the threat caused by the West, and for liberation on its own steam.

An important event for the church also occurred during "the time of troubles," namely, the establishment of the patriarchy in 1589. It was promulgated by the patriarch of Constantinople during his stay in Moscow. The hitherto four patriarchies of Constantinople, Alexandria, Antioch, and Jerusalem were all in the Ottoman Empire. They were financially dependent, above all, on Moscow, but also on Orthodox princes in Moldavia and Walachia. That is why many bishops came again and again to Russia with requests for financial support; Russia was the only independent Orthodox country. Now when the patriarch with the highest rank, the one from Constantinople, was in Moscow, Boris Godunov persuaded him to designate the Moscow metropolitan as patriarch. This put the Russian Church on one hierarchical level with the other aforementioned

Orthodox churches. The circumstances were the same as they were in the Byzantine Empire, namely, an autocratic ruler with an autocephalous church, headed by a patriarch.

In the seventeenth century, the tension between "old" and "new" became even more evident when Tsar Alexey attempted to revise the liturgical books according to the Greek originals. Many variations and mistakes had crept into the books, and the art of printing had made it possible to standardize the books. The project was begun during the middle of the century after some earlier, hesitating attempts. But there was intensive resistance, generated by a priest named Avvakum and his disciples. The content of the reforms had little theological weight. At stake was, above all, how to make the sign of the cross, the manner of writing the name Jesus, the direction of processions (turning toward the sun or away from it), and the number of "hallelujah's" in the liturgy (two or three). On the one hand, these liturgical customs established identity: personal faith was strengthened by rites, and any change of them would have to be viewed as an impairment of faith itself; one saw an indissoluble connection between the expression and the content of faith. On the other hand, making the sign of the cross imposed a change of behavior on every single believer; it, therefore, demanded the active cooperation of all members of the church. So the reforms led to a big schism. The "Old Believers," or more precisely, the "Old Ritualists," separated themselves from the church at large in 1667. This process cost many lives because church and state severely persecuted the Old Believers. Thousands of them chose martyrdom rather than making the sign of the cross incorrectly. In the background there was resistance against everything "Western," and also against deplorable social conditions. Avvakum was excommunicated, several times exiled, and finally executed. Nevertheless, the Old Believers, who had split into many groups, endured and still exist today. The physical expanse of Russia allowed them to find places of refuge where they could remain undisturbed. Moreover, their economic significance, above all, as merchants, made it less attractive in the end for the state to proceed against them. But discriminations against them were stopped only after centuries.

An indirect consequence of the quarrel with the Old Believers was a conflict between the patriarch and the tsar. It resulted in the dismissal of Patriarch Nikon. One of his predecessors, Patriarch Filaret, had been the father of the first Romanov tsar with great political influence. Nikon, however, did not succeed in enacting his idea that the patriarch held a higher position than the tsar. The reversal of the two positions was to determine the life of Russian Orthodoxy for the next centuries — the tsar was the highest position in the state, and finally also in the church. The church had to be subordinate to the interests of the state.

The Reforms of Peter the Great and the Synodical Phase

The next great epoch of Russian history and church history is linked to the city of St. Petersburg. Tsar Peter I ("the Great") founded it in 1703 and gave it a symbolic Latin-German name (originally Latin-Dutch). In this manner, he elucidated his goal: to orient Russia toward the West and to reorganize the state and society according to western European models. This is shown in the numerous details of public administration, of the military, and of public life, as well as with regard to the Orthodox Church and the relationship with non-Orthodox religious communities in Russia.

Like all reforms and developments of this kind, those named after Peter were prepared for beforehand. Already at the end of the seventeenth century, above all under Tsar Fyodor, there had been efforts at reform. One influence came to Moscow from the south: since 1667, one part of Ukraine belonged to Russia (the "left bank Ukraine," that is, the regions located east of the river Dnepr, together with the city of Kiev). Moreover, strengthened Western ideas came to Moscow from those areas that had long belonged to Poland and Lithuania. But already long before, Orthodox theologians had been brought from Kiev to Russia. While Western influence came later to Russia directly from western European countries, under and after Peter I, Ukraine played a mediating role during this preparatory phase. Since 1632, there was the Kiev College (*Collegium Kioviense* in Latin); later it became an ecclesiastical academy. Orthodoxy in Ukraine tried to protect itself against Roman Catholicism through improved education and a systematizing of its theology. But in the process, it frequently accepted the methods of the Catholic Church and its theology. Especially, Peter Mogila must be mentioned here. He was active in the first half of the seventeenth century and became the metropolitan of Kiev. Although Orthodox theologians from Kiev aroused suspicion in Moscow, because contacts with Catholic Poles were often distrusted, ideas, shaped by the West, still reached Moscow by way of Kiev because a number of theologians from Kiev had been educated at Polish institutions, or even in Rome.

This was the situation when Peter came to power in 1689 after some dynastic quarrels. He put numerous administrative reforms into action. In his foreign policy, he turned toward the Baltic Sea. In campaigns against Sweden, he conquered the area where St. Petersburg was later located, thus creating Russia's access to the Baltic Sea. By reforming the army and creating a navy, he was able in a short time to enlarge and secure the Russian territory. Internally, there were administrative reforms, especially with regard to taxation; the tax system became more effective and produced a surplus needed for the military enterprises.

Peter's reforms were far-reaching with regard to the church. When Patriarch Adrian died in 1700, the tsar prevented a quick new election. The office of the patriarch was dissolved, and Metropolitan Stefan Yavorskiy was appointed to administer the position. Yavorskiy came from Ukraine and favored Peter's ideas that were imbued with the strivings of the European Enlightenment. The deceased patriarch and his predecessors had been highly skeptical toward such innovations. The tsar was aware that the conservative high clergy and its ties to the wealth of the church were an obstacle to his policies. So he tried to neutralize both. The "monastic office" was founded once again. As a secular authority, it was to see to it that the state received the profit from the real estate of the monasteries and that later all land owned by the church would become state property. With the office of the patriarch being abolished, after a vacancy of some duration the control of the church was handed over to the Most Holy Governing Synod, a governing body consisting of bishops. But the synod had a state officer at its side (who later became its de facto head), the chief procurator. This synod was a part of the public administration. The church was integrated into the state and was consequently deprived of its independence. The theological basis of these measures was stated in a document titled "Spiritual Regulation."[3] It was published in 1721 and authored by the head of the Kiev Academy, Feofan Prokopovich. He had come to know Western theology while studying in Rome. He also adopted some Protestant principles. In this way, he tried to make Orthodox traditions suitable for his own time through the application of Western methods and principles.

The state had absolute control of the church, since the office of the chief procurator was given ever more power. The entire correspondence

3. English translation: Alexander V. Muller, ed., *The Spiritual Regulation of Peter the Great* (Seattle: University of Washington Press, 1972).

of the bishops had to be conducted through the synod, which was a simple means of control. Peter also decreed that the synod was to be mentioned in the liturgy.

How much Peter was impressed by Western, above all, Protestant models also in church administration is evident in many details: the introduction of a collective guidance of the church; the fact that German and Latin words became foreign terms in Russian *(reglament, ober-prokuror);* the adoption of the Julian calendar, which substituted the customary calculation "since the creation of the world" with the beginning of the year in September. European Enlightenment convictions were in the background, calling for the common good to determine statesmanship. Another expression of this stance is the reform of monasticism in 1722/24. It restricted entrance into a monastery and demanded concentration on activities judged to be useful.

The notion of the common good also included an educational assignment for the church. It referred less to concrete education than to cooperation in the formation of the population for public purposes, namely, those of the state. Among them were educational institutions in the dioceses or systematic training of the clergy to improve the educational standard of priests. Since it was not possible to create quickly an encompassing, common educational system, the attempt was made to influence believers through priests. Two models were developed, one in the Moscow Academy, striving for a Latinized, primarily ecclesiastical-theological education, headed by Yavorskiy; and the opposite model of the Boarding School of Prokopovich in St. Petersburg, where secular subjects dominated.

Although Peter had founded an academy, theology was soon put under the control of the synod. Scientific theology became isolated from other subjects because it had its own schools and monasteries. There was no traditional university *(universitas litterarum)* that included theology. Besides, the first university was founded in 1755. This was a momentous development that resulted, first of all, in making monasteries the locations for theological education. Consequently, scientific theological work was very much isolated from other intellectual developments in the country. This arrangement was basically not different in the Soviet Union, and still today, many Russian theologians have first finished another education; they were natural scientists or graduates of the humanities before they turned to theology.

The endeavor to use religion primarily for the common good also includes Peter's attitude toward the Old Believers and the adherents of other religions. The Old Believers were no longer persecuted and exiled, but they had to pay significantly higher taxes. The non-Orthodox Christians in Russia were foreigners whom Peter I had brought into the country. Their pastors could also come to Russia. But, of course, they were only allowed to care for their own believers, and missionary endeavors were strictly prohibited.

When Peter I died in 1725, he left behind a totally different empire than the one he began with: a great power that had, within a few decades, become an important factor within the European balance of power. Inward, the empire was marked by ideas of the European Enlightenment, with a church that was basically skeptical toward the new changes but could not do much about them. In the subsequent centuries, every activity of the church was judged by its relation to the common good, that is, the well-being of the state. It is not surprising that conservative representatives of the church, in part, consider Peter an embodiment of the Antichrist, making Russia accessible to many harmful and destructive influences. So he is viewed in contrast to Tsar Ivan IV ("the Terrible"), who tried to construct the state with Russian values and tradition. Here, too, the basic conflict between "old" and "new" emerges once again. It remains unsolved still today.

In the eighteenth century, the influence of the European Enlightenment, begun by Peter, continued in principle. Until the time of Catherine II ("the Great," who ruled after 1762), several male and female rulers succeeded one another. Today, they are assessed in different ways, but none of them made basic course corrections. In the brief reign of Catherine's predecessor, Peter III, monastic property was confiscated and delivered to the state. Moreover, the demotion of the non-Orthodox religious communities also stopped, as did the discriminating taxation of the Old Believers. Under Catherine's absolutistic rule, grounded in the European Enlightenment, even foreigners were expressly invited to settle in Russia; the Russian Germans can be traced to the settlers who had accepted the invitation.

The turn to the European Enlightenment — also again and again retracted — was at its height during the reign of Catherine. It continued to marginalize the church in society. The church, of course, was viewed as a self-evident part of Russia. But it was not a self-reliant institution, able to act independently. It was powerless against the mandates of secularization; it had to endure the immigration of non-Orthodox people; it could do nothing against the ideas of the Enlightenment at the imperial court; and it was totally dependent on the chief procurator, that is, in the final analysis, on the tsar. Although the educational level of priests had increased since Peter, there was hardly any pastoral activity beyond the celebration of the sacraments. The office of the priest was often inherited, above all in the villages, and was passed on from father to son. Alcoholism seems to have been a widespread phenomenon among the clergy.

However, there came to be a certain concentration on academic theology, which blossomed in the nineteenth century. This was a consequence of the development that did not allow the church to engage actively in society. Above all, the historical disciplines produced significant efforts, not only in Russian church history but also generally in Oriental church history. Furthermore, the philosophy of religion flowered after the middle of the nineteenth century.

During the nineteenth century nationalism and national consciousness increased in eastern Europe. This topic is also of central importance for Russia. By the end of the nineteenth century, only 44 percent of the population were ethnic Russians. Ukrainians, at 18 percent, and Poles, at 6 percent, were the largest non-Russian nations within Russia; about 12 percent of the population were Muslims, among whom almost all missionary attempts had failed. Among them, as well as among other nations, there arose the consciousness of becoming suppressed by Russia. The Orthodox Church was perceived as Russian and as an organization that supported the suppression and favored the Russification. As a matter of fact, since the nineteenth century only ethnic Russians were instituted as metropolitans of Kiev (before, until the middle of the eighteenth century, many hierarchs who headed dioceses in Russia came from Ukraine). The Ukrainian national movement, originating in Hapsburg Galicia, extended only slowly to the eastern part of the country. In Georgia, the Orthodox Church was confronted with the attempt of a complete Russification ever since Georgia had fallen to Russia in 1811. Since 1817, only Russians were nominated to be "Catholicos" (the title of the head of Georgian Orthodoxy), and Russian became the language for liturgy and teaching. Only in the Soviet Union could the Georgian church again use its own language.

So Russian Orthodoxy was in an extremely difficult situation when it had to face probably the most powerful challenges in its history. It was a vast organization to which the majority of the population belonged, but without any real power; it was almost completely isolated from the Russian intelligentsia; and it consisted of a hierarchy without contact with the believers. The emerging industrialization and the modernization linked to it created numerous problems for the country, as did the national question. But the church was not viewed as being in a position to offer solutions for these manifold problems, or even to lend assistance. It was regarded as part of the system, and not wrongly so. Here, the tight institutionalized connection of the church with the state since Peter I showed its consequences.

The Twentieth Century

The revolutions of 1917 also did not come totally unexpectedly. Already in 1905, there was an attempt on the political level to move the system to make concessions; but without any success. In the church, one could hear calls, above all, for the reestablishment of the patriarchy; but the calls also failed. Many bishops realized that ecclesiastical reforms were absolutely necessary. For a brief time it looked as if the tsar would permit a local council to decide these issues. In 1917, Russia became de facto a republic: the tsar abdicated in the first revolution (February/March), and a "provisional government" took over. It was swept away in the October revolution when the "majority party" *(Bolsheviki)* took control of the capital and soon also of the country. All this happened in an atmosphere of strikes, demonstrations, and uprisings, of constantly changing governments, internal quarrels between the participating groups, and, not least, a world war.

The provisional government tried to bring about democratic reforms as fast as possible. The national minorities were to get their rights, which were also shared by other religious communities besides the Orthodox Church (the most discriminating measures against the national minorities had been removed already in 1905). This had far-reaching consequences for Orthodoxy. During the summer of 1917, parishes and priests were given greater autonomy over against the bishops who were to be assisted by a "diocesan governing body." The ministry of education had control of the 37,000 ecclesiastical schools, and freedom of religion was determined by law. The office of the chief procurator was abolished. A newly instituted ministry for confessions of faith regarded the Orthodox Church as an autonomous corporation. It was now in a position, perhaps for the first time, to settle its own affairs.

Given this situation, the church decided to convene a local council to decide, above all, whether or not to reestablish the patriarchal office but also to initiate necessary reforms. Sanctioned by the government, the council met in the Kremlin on August 15, 1917. Since such a council had been already demanded during the revolutionary efforts in 1905 (and had been approved but was never convened), one could refer to the preparations made at that time. The council was able to act with a freedom never known before. The laity constituted the majority among the 564 members, including all the bishops. However, it was made possible for the bishops to reject decisions of the council if they voted with great unanimity. So the principle of Orthodox ecclesiology was preserved, according to which the episcopal office was the basis of the church. But the participating delegates had far-reaching rights.

After long discussions, the council decided on November 4, virtually the same date as the revolution, to reestablish the patriarchy. The local council was designated to be the supreme ecclesiastical organ. The patriarch had an accentuated role among the bishops but was accountable to the council. The metropolitan of Moscow, Tikhon (Belavin), was appointed to be the first patriarch and was solemnly enthroned on November 21. This event ended the synodical phase of Russian church history.

But this was also the beginning of an extremely difficult phase of Russian church history, the persecution during Communism. Circumstances prevented the realization of the council's numerous decisions.[4] Foremost among them was the application of the synodical principle on all levels of the church, with an institutionalized influence of the laity, for example, in the election of bishops. The council contained a powerful theological and ecclesiastical potential that had hardly been used. For the time being, there also seemed to be no desire in the Russian Church to have recourse to it.

Repression by the new rulers began very quickly. On December 2, all ecclesiastical property was nationalized, and a few days later all schools were transferred to the state. On January 20, 1918, the famous "Decree on Freedom of Conscience, Religious and Ecclesiastical Associations"[5] origi-

4. See, above all, Günter Schulz, Gisela A. Schröder, and C. Timm Richter, *Bolschewistische Herrschaft und Orthodoxe Kirche in Russland. Das Landeskonzil 1917-18. Quellen und Analysen* (Münster: LIT, 2005); Hyacinthe Destivelle, *Le Concile de Moscou (1917-1918). La création des institutions conciliaires de l'Église orthodoxe russe* (Paris, 2006).

5. English text: Dimitry V. Pospielovsky, *A History of Marxist-Leninist Atheism and Soviet Antireligious Policies* (New York: St. Martin's Press, 1987), 134-35.

nated. Its first section was to read: "religion is the personal affair of every citizen of the Russian Republic," but Lenin replaced the section in his own handwriting with the sentence: "the church is separated from the state." This sentence really expressed the greatest problem of Russian Orthodoxy over many centuries. But it did not solve it, especially since the new rulers themselves did not adhere to it but in various ways exercised control over the church. Nevertheless, the principle of the separation of church and state remained officially the maxim of all Soviet ecclesiastical politics. On paper, religion was a private affair; but freedom of religion was, above all, understood as freedom from religion.

The decree also enacted the separation of church and school, prohibiting any religious instruction. The ecclesiastical communities were viewed as private associations. They were not permitted to have any property nor the rights of corporations. All ecclesiastical buildings became property of the state and were made available to the believers. Action of the state had to proceed without any religious ceremonies. Registers of births, marriages, and deaths were taken over by the state. These incisive measures were to terminate the anchorage of the church in the population and earlier competencies of the church in the public sphere.

The first reaction of the church consisted in the excommunication of the Bolsheviks on January 19, 1918: "by our authority, granted by God, we prohibit you from the access to the sacraments of Christ and declare the anathema over you."[6] It goes without saying that this made little impression on the new rulers. On the other hand, the patriarch and the council viewed the Communist government only as a transition. They assumed that sooner or later a legitimate government would prevail. That is why large parts of the church supported the "Whites," that is, the opponents of the Bolsheviks. The church organized mass protests of believers. The initial reaction of the regime was flexible in order not to provoke a scandal. In January of 1918 the metropolitan of Kiev was shot as the first of thousands of martyrs.

A systematic persecution of churches occurred in the early 1920s. It began with the refusal of the church to offer consecrated liturgical objects for sale to ease the famine. The state confiscated the objects by force, and the public propaganda increased. Many priests, as well as bish-

---

6. From a letter of the newly elected patriarch, in Peter Hauptmann and Gerd Stricker, eds., *Die Orthodoxe Kirche in Russland. Dokumente ihrer Geschichte (860-1980)* (Göttingen: Vandenhoeck & Ruprecht, 1988), 646.

ops, were sentenced and imprisoned, or executed. Between 1917 and 1922, 2,691 priests, 1,962 monks, and 3,447 nuns were condemned to death and executed. In addition, many were killed without a verdict (about 15,000).[7] A few dozen bishops met their death. Out of more than 1,000 monasteries, 700 were closed. A camp for clergymen was established on the Solovki Islands in the White Sea. In 1921, the synod consisted of only two rather than thirteen members. Patriarch Tikhon was put under house arrest and later jailed for a year.

The state also tried to weaken the church by initiating schisms. Since some clergymen sympathized with the Bolsheviks and demanded extensive reforms in the realm of discipline for the clergy and in the liturgy, they were given an opportunity to take over the guidance of the orphaned patriarchy. But these so-called Renewers were not trusted by the believers even though they had the full support of the state. Another schism, which could not be influenced by the state, happened abroad. Most of the bishops, who had fled during the disturbances caused by the civil war, established a synod of their own. Although it basically acknowledged Tikhon, it viewed itself as independent of Moscow in its affairs until the Soviet government came to an end and the church became free once again.

In 1923 a "Declaration of Repentance" was published by Patriarch Tikhon. In it he confessed that he would no longer be an enemy of the Soviet reign. Its authenticity is as disputed as that of his testament that was published after his death in 1925. He seems to have made an attempt to reach a consensus with the Soviet rulers. After his death, no local council could convene to elect a successor. He had designated three administrators for the office in his will, but all three soon lost their ability to act. The third one had been able to create a list of designated successors. But, again, only the third, Metropolitan Sergiy (Stragorodskiy), remained free and able to lead the church. Together with some other bishops, he established a "preliminary synod," and in 1927 he published a disputed declaration in which he expressed the loyalty of the church to the Soviet Union.[8]

---

7. See Gerd Stricker, *Religion in Russland. Darstellung und Daten zu Geschichte und Gegenwart* (Gütersloh: Gütersloher Verlagshaus, 1993), 86.

8. English translation: Declaration of Loyalty by Metropolitan Sergius, in Paul D. Steeves, ed., *The Modern Encyclopedia of Religions in Russia and Soviet Union*, vol. 6 (Gulf Breeze, Fla.: Academic International Press, 1995), 242-46. The central sentence reads (p. 244): "We want to be Orthodox and at the same time to recognize the Soviet Union as our civil motherland, whose joys and successes are our joys and successes and whose misfortunes are our misfortunes."

But this declaration did nothing to prevent the increase of persecutions of the church. The relatively liberal stance in the realm of culture lasted until the late 1920s, the dawn of the Stalin regime. This did not just extend to the church. When a census showed that there still were many believers, the battle against religion increased. The "Movement of the Godless" and the "Militant Atheists" campaigned for the liquidation of religion. Feast days became normal working days. In 1929 a five-year plan was passed; at its conclusion, there were to be no longer any outward manifestations of religion. Since all areas of life in the country were controlled, any religious engagement was also controlled. Moreover, the church lost the rural population through the establishment of collective farms in villages *(kolkhozes)* and agricultural centers in the country *(sovkhozes)*. Ecclesiastical activity was reduced to the realm of worship. Possibilities for catechesis were radically limited. Moreover, representatives of the church were forced to forswear any form of persecution. This measure was aimed, above all, at the perception of the Bolshevik regime abroad.

The general terror in the second half of the 1930s also struck the church, and the patriarchal church as well as the "Renewers." Not only the intelligentsia and the military authorities, but also almost the entire clergy, fell victim to the "purges." In 1943, there were only 4 acting bishops, over against 160 hierarchs in 1914. All monasteries and educational institutions were closed; the church could not produce anything in print; and only 500 of the more than 50,000 churches in the country were utilized. The Orthodox Church in Russia had, in fact, come close to its end.

Church leaders, now extremely limited in their opportunities to act, tried to reach some compromise with their rulers. This proved impossible. In the church, there were also groups who disapproved this course of the last remaining hierarchs and went underground to resist the hated regime, or to live their faith in isolation. It is almost impossible to ascertain how many individuals acted accordingly and how long these groups could endure. But it is known that this phenomenon existed.

The situation of the church changed fundamentally in World War II. After the German military assault on the Soviet Union, Metropolitan Sergiy immediately summoned all believers to resist. So in the face of the German attack the church supported a state that had almost completely destroyed it. This shows how significant the state as the homeland of the Russian nation was for the Orthodox Church regardless of its attitude to the church. The concrete manifestation of this support of the church was a collection to finance weapons for the Red Army.

The state rewarded this attitude by moving toward the church and making some concessions. Other circumstances, however, also played a role in the territories occupied by the Germans. Churches were again reopened; a hierarchy was installed; and the population greeted the occupants at some locations as the ones who had brought freedom of religion. The leadership of the USSR now noticed that its measures of persecution were counterproductive. In 1943 Stalin met with Metropolitan Sergiy and two bishops, and he approved the convocation of the local council. This council elected Sergiy as patriarch after a vacancy of eighteen years. Moreover, after his death in the subsequent year, a successor could be chosen by another council.

At the end of the war, the Soviet religious policy was reorganized. A Council on the Russian Orthodox Church Affairs (later called "Council for Religious Affairs") was established. It was dependent on the Council of Ministers of the USSR. These institutions, which had offices also in republics and provinces, were instruments of control, but also partners of dialogue for the church. Now the church could again open some seminaries and publish a periodical. Ecclesiastical life began to develop slowly; the number of parishes and priests increased gradually. Religious life blossomed especially in the formerly Polish territories that had been occupied by the Germans and became part of the USSR after the war. Due to the changed religious policy, the churches were not immediately closed there but could — at least for some time — remain open. The Greek Catholic ("Uniate") Church in the western Ukraine was an exception; after 1946, it and all its property were incorporated by force into the Orthodox Church.

Now the church had somewhat greater control over its internal affairs. The indiscriminate measures of persecution and the terror stopped. As long as the church observed its own boundaries, imposed by the state, it could act. Now, the state attempted to proceed against the church with administrative measures. A fundamental condemnation of the World Council of Churches (WCC) in 1948 preceded the Russian Orthodox Church joining the WCC in 1961. Both events could not occur without the knowledge and approval of the state. But both also had supporters in the church. Acknowledging, in principle, the prerogatives of the state, some bishops were experts in using the free spaces for the church as far as possible. Other bishops kept back and, eager to obey, did nothing but what government officials presumably would allow. The state, on its side, reacted against citizens whose engagement with the church was "too" strong (especially when they appealed to freedom of religion and attracted international attention). For disliked priests and bishops, attempts were made to obtain, for the most part, an ecclesiastical punishment. The Soviet Secret Service (KGB) not only had its informers among church members but also occasionally channeled agents into the hierarchy.

The so-called de-Stalinization, begun under Nikita Khrushchev in 1956, led to a harsher course toward the church. To some extent, it is to be understood as a balance. In the period of "the thaw,"[9] many parishes were closed and "too" active hierarchs were pensioned off. The state now intensified its attempts to use the church also for advances in foreign policy. Themes of peace and disarmament had to be on the agenda at all ecumenical encounters. Today, this is judged controversially; but it is inadequate if the concentration of the church on the question of peace is only viewed as a success of the KGB.

Until the 1980s, the phenomenon can be observed that the rare and cautious openings in society were accompanied by restrictions of ecclesiastical activities. Even though the state had extensive control over the church, time and again something aroused suspicion and prompted the state to take steps against it, such as demands for religious freedom by priests and laypeople, who then had to endure coercive measures.

There was no sustained change in the relation between church and state until the time of *perestroika* (restructuring). Its clearest sign was the millenarian celebration of the Christianization of the Rus' in 1988. The church could organize festivities in cooperation with public authorities; it was taken seriously as a partner in dialogue; and the public regulations have disappeared since then.

At the end of 1991 the Soviet Union was dissolved, and the Russian Federation became its largest successor state. The public value of the ROC over against political institutions has been considerably raised. It is an influential factor in the nation and has great significance for the formation of a Russian identity after the end of the Soviet identity. This was especially important at a time when previously significant values had lost their validity.

But the situation is also problematic. After 1991, many of the same actors remained. Patriarch Pimen (Izvekov), a representative of the Brezhnev era, which is called today, not wrongly, a "time of stagnation," died in

9. The title of a novel by the Russian writer Ilya Erenburg (1954).

1990. His successor, Alexiy II (Ridiger), could begin his office without any extensive compromising reproaches. But many bishops who received their ecclesiastical position with the sanction of the Soviet authorities still exercise their office today. And even though these hierarchs are no longer incriminated, they often constitute a psychological barrier for the critical debate about the role of the church in the time of the Soviets. Such a debate has not yet occurred, be it in the public or any other social domain.

Today, a further problem is the realization of the freedom of religion. This means for Russia that not only other churches can exist in the country (the Roman Catholic Church established hierarchical structures, resented by Russian Orthodoxy), but even "sects" and new religious movements can operate in Russia. Ordinarily, their efforts are largely unsuccessful. But they are a thorn in the flesh of the Orthodox Church because they are in conflict with the image of Russia as an Orthodox country. While there was a liberal law for religion toward the end of the *perestroika*, a stronger law with more regulations was passed in 1997, not without the sanction of the Orthodox Church. However, it favors the traditional religious communities, which are Orthodoxy, Islam, Judaism, and Buddhism.

But the revaluation of the role of the church in society does not mean that it has already found its place there. This has to do with its political choices (in the coups of 1991 and 1993 the hierarchs of the church were always on both sides), and also with its attitude toward human rights and civil liberties. It is equally evident that the extensive approval and appreciation enjoyed by the Orthodox Church in Russia is not matched in the same measure by religiosity. Many value the church as an institution but do not "use" it for their own lives.

CHAPTER THREE

Christianization and Expansion

T his chapter deals with the question of how Christianity came to the Rus' and expanded. The question of the expansion also includes the topic of the Russian dispersion, above all, in the twentieth century. It is not only of great importance for Orthodox church history but also for the perception of Russian Orthodoxy and for the dissemination of Russian theological ideas and beginnings in the West.

The "baptism of the Rus'" is commonly assigned to the year 988, and good reasons can be cited that this is correct. But there is no absolute certainty. The Finnish historian Korpela writes that 988 is considered the year of the baptism because the Russian imperial government decided to celebrate the 900th anniversary in 1888.[1] Even though this opinion may not be shared, it points to an important phenomenon: the baptism of the Rus' was given the significance it has today only after it occurred. Here, a basic problem appears and needs to be briefly addressed: every view of the past is respectively always a construction of its own and is never an "objective" reconstruction of "how it really was." This is especially important when historical events are used to justify specific interests or later phenomena. It is quite obvious that the Christianization of a "people" is especially well suited for such a purpose. Other nations also like to make an appeal to events and persons. History is not a linear process whose result allows inspection in the present but a reaching back for events and

1. Jukka Korpela, *Prince, Saint, and Apostle: Prince Vladimir Svjatoslavic of Kiev, His Posthumous Life, and the Religious Legitimization of the Russian Great Power* (Wiesbaden: Harrassowitz, 2001), 12.

developments that, in each case, are newly constructed and differently interpreted. Consequently, their interpretation is always disputed, especially in regard to spaces and times defined by discontinuities. But the Christianization of the Rus' was not only a new beginning. It also had numerous elements of continuity, first with the acting persons, the rulers as well the subjects who, indeed, were the same, then via the topography all the way to the political constellation that, however, also showed something new in its rapprochement to Byzantium. There was, to be sure, no great difference in the daily rounds of people. Christianity made its way only slowly. The reports of chronicles, written by monks, must be read with critical caution. For they were interested in depicting the progress of the true faith as convincingly as possible and reported about quick successes.

The example of the baptism of the Rus' also shows that historical assertions can frequently become explosive in the present. This becomes evident in the quest for the influence of the Norman Varangians: What role did they play in the formation of political power structures in the Rus'? Were they representatives of a relatively thin layer of the elite, or had there been a larger migration from Scandinavia to Kiev? How is one to judge the assertions of the chronicle that the inhabitants of the Rus' had called the Varangians to create order in their land since they themselves could not do it? It is clear that the answers to these questions are not only an interpretation of the assertions discovered in the sources but that also political intentions can be connected with the event. If there are ideological handicaps for the understanding of history, as they existed in the Soviet period, then more is read into the sources than what is in them. This hermeneutical problem has to be faced in every historical presentation. On this background, the witticism of Soviet historians makes sense: "It is so difficult to predict the past."

Early Christianity before the "Baptism of the Rus'"

Slavic tribes appear in historical sources with various descriptions. Their original home is probably in what is today northwestern Ukraine. During the migration period they spread over territories to the west, the north, and the southeast of their original home. This process can be somewhat reconstructed through names of locations and of waters as well as through the development of language in the individual Slavic languages.

In the Byzantine sources, the Slavs are mentioned after the sixth century. In those sources, as well as in some late antique authors, various designations, such as "Wends," "Antes," or "Sclavins," are used for them. Later, the name Rhos appears in the Byzantine writings, designating northern neighbors. Since the Black Sea area belonged to the sphere of interest of Constantinople, and also probably because monks established hermitages at its northern shore, these people had contacts with Christianity, but also conflicts with Byzantium. The name Rhos surfaces first in 839 when residents of the Rhos appear in a Byzantine embassy in Ingelheim, a place on the Rhine. Emperor Louis the Pious investigated their origin and "ascertained that they belonged to the nation of the Swedes."[2] In the ninth century, reports accumulate about raids of the Rus' against Greek cities, finally in 860 even against Constantinople. So the emperors there had reasons to act in order to stabilize their relations with their northern neighbor. At this time, Kiev also seems to form itself as the center of the Rus'. It is evident that the Varangians established an economic and political center in fortified Kiev while searching for a water route from Scandinavia to the Black Sea and thus to Constantinople.

The residents of the Rus', to be sure, worshiped gods of nature who belonged to a pantheon familiar to the Slavs. A Greek source reports a Christianization in the ninth century. But it did not endure, possibly quenched by the immigration of new Varangians. The first reliable information comes from the middle of the tenth century. A church in Kiev is mentioned in 944-45. After the death of Prince Ingvar (*Igor* in Slavic), his widow Olga *(Helga)* took over the regency of the underage son, Svyatoslav — a Slavic name without a Scandinavian equivalent, evidence of the penetration into the upper class by Slavs. Olga agreed to be baptized around 954-55 and also tried to acquire a bishop for the Rus' during a stay in Constantinople. Likewise, she also made contact with the western emperor Otto I, but without lasting success. After her death, these beginnings of Christianity in Kiev again expired. Svyatoslav was critical of his mother's efforts and did not support her. Even though the beginnings of Christianity were lost, they were remembered, and the authors of the chronicles still know of them.

---

2. Ludolf Müller, *Die Taufe Russlands. Die Frühgeschichte des russischen Christentums bis zum Jahre 988* (Munich: Wewel, 1987), 19.

Christianization

Svyatoslav's son Vladimir became sole ruler in 980 after he had eliminated his brothers, and he was able to expand his rule. In the summer of 987 the Byzantine emperor Basileios II asked Vladimir for military help. He had suffered a heavy defeat by the Bulgarians and, in addition, had come into conflict with two opposing emperors. As a reward, he offered his sister Anna as a wife. With his offer, he could not only secure the assistance of the Rus' but also tie dynastic bonds. Although this did not prevent further campaigns against Constantinople, it made them less probable. But the emperor made his offer to the Kiev prince under condition of baptism. His sister, "purple-born," that is, an offspring of the imperial palace in Constantinople, could not be given in marriage to a pagan. Vladimir consented, was probably baptized in 988, and sent soldiers who successfully assisted the emperor. At the same time, the princess came to Kiev and became his wife. According to reports, probably during the same summer of 988 a mass baptism of the population occurred in the river Dnepr. The reports presumably indicate the efforts to spread the new faith quickly. The statues of the old gods in Kiev were dismantled, and a stone church was built in the city. Since the campaigns against the two pretenders to the throne ended with success, the power of the Byzantine emperor was stabilized in the time to come.

This, then, is the account of events as they can be somewhat reliably presented. Ludolf Müller summarized them with a critical sifting of the sources and with respect to Andrzej Poppe.[3] A consideration of these sources clearly shows that the account is quite differentiated. The best-known text is certainly the so-called Nestor's Chronicle, in which Vladimir sends envoys to the neighboring peoples to gather information about their religion. After they return, they report.

When we journeyed among the Bulgars, we beheld how they worship in their temple, called a mosque, while they stand ungirt. The Bulgar bows, sits down, looks hither and thither like one possessed, and there is no happiness among them but instead only sorrow and a dreadful stench. Their religion is not good. Then we went among the Germans, and saw them performing many ceremonies in their temples; but we beheld no glory there. Then we went to Greece, and the Greeks led us

3. Müller, *Die Taufe Russlands*, 16.

to the edifices where they worship their God; and we knew not whether we were in heaven or earth. For on earth there is no such splendor or such beauty.[4]

The entire context of this narrative, in which the reports about Islam and Western Christianity turn out be negative, has a legendary character. Yet Nestor's Chronicle was considered for a long time an authentic description of what had taken place. Noteworthy is the category of "beauty." It plays a decisive role in the negative judgment about "German" (Latin) Christianity as well as in the positive evaluation of the faith of the Greeks. An aesthetic, surely not an intellectual, criterion identifies the right, the true religion. Other elements of the chronicle have a historical core, such as the establishment of relations to the Byzantine imperial family and the Christianity of Vladimir's grandmother Olga; they are mentioned later in the text. The author of the report in the chronicle that originated at the turn from the eleventh to the twelfth century linked his account with the intention to show the Christianization of the Rus' as a conscious decision for the best religion after other possibilities had been considered.

There are a number of other accounts about how the acceptance of Christianity in Kiev occurred. They range from "Andrew's Legend," claiming that the apostle preached the gospel already in the first century at the place where Kiev was to arise, to an Arabic account from the first half of the eleventh century that presents a short sequence of historical events that is perhaps the most correct one.

A critical analysis of the accounts discloses the increasing significance of the Rus', evident in trade relations, but also in warlike conflicts, and the mutually sensed need for the incorporation of the Rus' into the system of power politics in the region. Moreover, the commitment to a dominant main religion was also necessary. Eastern Christianity was geographically close, but Islam and, with restriction, Latin Christianity would also have been realistic options. When earlier attempts of Christianization — always by the ruling class — were unsuccessful, the distressed situation of the Byzantine emperor and the need of Prince Vladimir for political revaluation met halfway near the end of the tenth century. There was no historical necessity forcing Vladimir to make his decision. But the conditions

---

4. English translation: Samuel Hazzard Cross and Olgerd P. Sherbowitz-Wetzor, trans. and ed., *The Russian Primary Chronicle, Laurentian Text* (Cambridge, Mass.: Mediaeval Academy of America, 1953), 111.

were favorable. "The time had become ripe for making his historical decision. That is why it lasted."[5]

It is quite understandable that the role of Vladimir was revalued later and positively portrayed. This positive view is probably correct only in a very modified way. After all, it is a question of a brother killing his brother and persecuting Christians, who accepted Christianity for reasons of power politics, not because he was convinced that the Christian faith was metaphysically correct. Nevertheless, the sources disclose the intention to portray the process of Christianization and its initiator in the best possible light. Moreover, the dynasty of Vladimir was in power when the chronicles were written. It goes without saying that the description of his depravity and mistakes was restrained. This is quite well demonstrated in the "Sermon on Law and Grace" by Metropolitan Ilarion, a eulogy for the grand prince given about 1050; it contributed decisively to his canonization in the thirteenth century.[6]

The logic of the incorporation of the Rus' into the community of the eastern Christian nations demanded the construction of an ecclesiastical structure that had to happen with assistance from Constantinople. The church of Kiev remained dependent on Constantinople; from there, it was managed as a metropolis, being sixtieth in the canonical sequence. The first historically verified metropolitan is Feopempt, mentioned in 1039. Catholic authors used this juridical vagueness of the first decades as an occasion to construct a dependence of the church of the Rus' on Rome. It is, however, completely improbable and is hardly still seriously advocated today. But this detail shows the kind of significance that could be allotted in the center of Western Christianity to a connection with the new factor of power in the East. This must also be seen in the context of the fact that the popes were interested very early in contacts with the Rus' and, perchance, had relations with the southwestern principalities (for example, Halich). The advance of the Teutonic Order two centuries later must also be seen as an attempt of the Western church to count "Russia" as part of its own sphere of influence. If the thesis of the original ecclesiastical affiliation of Kiev with Rome could be maintained, it would be a further argument that Russia "really" should be Catholic. Here we see the problem of using historical arguments for consequences in the present.

---

5. Müller, *Die Taufe Russlands*, 115.

6. Simon Franklin, ed., *Sermons and Rhetoric from Kievan Rus'* (Cambridge, Mass.: Ukrainian Research Institute of Harvard University, 1991), 3-29.

The schism of 1054 also opposes a narrower relation with Rome. First, it had few concrete consequences in the entire world of Eastern Christianity. Only in the course of subsequent decades, indeed centuries, did the separation become a reality everywhere. But the church of Kiev also had received reserves from Constantinople that existed already before 1054 opposite Latin Christianity.

In consequence of the juridical dependence on Greece, many influences from there gained acceptance in Kiev. Ecclesiastical and theological literature was translated from the Greek; besides the Gospels, liturgical books were translated because they were, of course, necessary as the liturgy was celebrated in the Slavic language. An indigenous literature also originated, besides the aforementioned chronicles and homilies, above all, stories of saints and martyrs as well as canonical regulations. Soviet scholarship always highlighted the independence of the old Russian literature. But it remained for a long time in the Greek tradition that it was accepted and fruitfully processed. Something similar can be said about the construction of churches, which was first under Greek influence but then also developed its own elements. The first church was completed in 996 and was dedicated to the Mother of God. The Saint Sophia Church in Kiev originated in 1037 as the cathedral of the city, in the style of the Hagia Sophia in Constantinople. But it was also an expression of the self-confidence that reigned in the Rus' over its own significance.

It is to be assumed that Christianization probably was limited first to the court, in the city of Kiev, as well as to the centers of other cities. But in the country, it penetrated only slowly. The "double faith" *(dvoyeveriye)* is extensively described as a problem. The chronicles speak several times of rebellious or obstinate pagan priests. Christianization came only gradually to the residents of the Rus'. But the Russian word for "peasant" *(krestyanin)* indicates that the settled farmers were understood to be Christian in the course of time, certainly also in contrast to the non-Christian, mostly Muslim, residents in the steppe.

Shift to the North

After the twelfth century, several power centers originated (Halich in the southwest, Novgorod in the northwest, Vladimir-Moscow in the north). With time, Halich seceded from the community of the Rus' principalities and subsequently turned toward the western countries of Poland and Lithuania. The two northern centers merged under the predominance of Moscow, and the once-so-significant Novgorod lost its greatness. Kiev no longer belonged to the "old" Rus', even though the Ukrainian, Polish-Lithuanian territories also called themselves Rus'. The "old" Rus' had shifted from the south to the north.

The interpretation of this process is extremely controversial in research. In particular, there is a Russian interpretation that is diametrically opposed by a Ukrainian one. According to the Russian view, it is a question of a "transfer of power" *(translatio imperii)* of the center of gravity of the Rus' from Kiev to the north, to Vladimir and finally to Moscow. According to this understanding, there is a direct continuity between the Kiev of the ninth century and the Moscow of the thirteenth century. But, according to the Ukrainian view, the continuity is valid for Kiev. That is why the northern developments since the twelfth century are independent and separate formations of power. They rely, to be sure, in part on Kiev, but have nothing in common with it. The history of the Kievan Rus' continues in Kiev, and continued for centuries under Polish and Lithuanian predominance. This dispute is ultimately still today the background for many quarrels between Russia and Ukraine.

There are good arguments in support of both positions. Some place-names had been transferred to the north from the south, indicating a migration and consequently a continuity as well as a transfer of political power. Today, most scholars are convinced that there was a reshaping of Finno-Ugric tribes residing in the north rather than a very massive migration. Prince Yuriy of Vladimir finally became grand prince of Kiev in 1155, but his son, who inherited the title, remained in Vladimir. This shows how important it was for the rulers of the northern cities to claim to be grand princes "of Kiev," independent of their actual residence. The metropolitan, to be sure, also took the Kiev title with him, pointing indeed to a "transfer of power." The plans of the metropolitan were excellently supplemented by a miraculous icon that seemed to confirm the decision to leave Kiev, since the approval of the Ecumenical Patriarch was not forthcoming.

But the history of the city of Kiev continued, even after its destruction by the Mongols in 1240. Orthodox metropolitans were there for some time so that two bishops claimed Kiev in their titles, one residing in Kiev and the other in Vladimir. By the seventeenth century, Orthodox ecclesiastical affairs were almost completely exhausted. But a historical continuity of Kiev can be developed from a Ukrainian perspective, disclosing not Russians but Poles and Lithuanians as the decisive factors. Here, a central role was played by the Union of Brest in 1595-96, when a part of the Orthodox Church in the Polish-Lithuanian kingdom entered into an ecclesiastical union with Rome. In 1620 an Orthodox metropolitan was again installed in Kiev, being in communion with the church in Moscow. So there were now two Orthodox communions that could claim continuity with Kiev, namely, the one in Kiev and the one in Moscow that traced its beginnings to Kiev. But the city of Kiev became part of Russia in 1627, and the diocese finally became a diocese within the Russian Church.

The rise of national consciousness in a modern sense, that is, in the nineteenth century, created two competing claims for continuity with Kiev. They are facing each other still today. Moreover, nothing militates basically against the point of view that, in the course of history, two traditions developed from the Christian beginnings in Kiev in the tenth century, and both still exist today. A problem arises only when the origins are viewed exclusively and when claims are derived from them. Since this is a presentation of the history of Russian Orthodoxy, it cannot produce a comprehensive inclusion of the other Kiev tradition.

The claim of the Kiev tradition by two sides causes again and again conflicts and differences of opinion. Among them is the millennial celebration of the baptism of Ukraine or of the Rus' by Ukrainian emigrants in 1988. On the other hand, an omnibus volume,[7] published by UNESCO in the same year, speaks of the Christianization "of Ancient Russia," even though the contributions speak always only of the Rus'. In the Soviet Union, the central celebration of the occasion did not take place in Kiev but in Moscow. All this indicates that the Rus' is claimed by Russians as well as by Ukrainians for their respective nations. But modern concepts of state and nation cannot be applied to the tenth century. Neither "Ukrainians" nor "Russians" were baptized in Kiev but only residents of the city, Slavs from the Rus', subjects of Prince Vladimir. Moreover, at that time the city was also not "capital of Ukraine,"[8] as it is stated in a Ukrainian volume published on the occasion of the millennial cele-

---

7. *The Christianization of Ancient Russia: A Millennium; 988-1988,* ed. Yves Hamant (Paris: UNESCO, 1992).

8. *Harvard Ukrainian Studies* 12-13 (Cambridge, Mass.: Harvard Ukrainian Research Institute Publications, 1988-89), 2. Preface by Omeljan Pritsak: "One thousand years ago . . . the kagan of the *Rus'* . . . decreed in Kiev, the capital of Ukraine. . . ."

bration. Rather, it was a center of power on the Dnepr that had become important and whose importance was to decrease again (and to increase again much later).

The shift of the center of power to the north was conditioned by the assault of the Mongols and by the loss of Kiev. That is why several sites gained political importance, in addition to being important from an ecclesiastical perspective. Since the country was already Christian, this development proceeded without any great attention with respect to the church. Consequently, one can speak only in a limited way of Christian expansion. On the other hand, the transfer of the metropolitan's residence is of great significance for the interpretation of the events.

The process of the "gathering of the Russian land," which began in Moscow in the fourteenth century, enjoyed also ecclesiastical assistance. Metropolitan Petr supported the grand prince of Moscow against the competing city of Tver. In 1325, the metropolitan moved his residency finally to Moscow. Grand Prince Ivan Kalita ("the Purse," who arranged the collection of tributes to the Golden Horde, the name given to the Mongolian empire) achieved the rise of Moscow by obtaining smaller principalities and also through the legitimacy that the transfer of the metropolitan's residence bestowed upon him. As a result, there was a growing dependence of the metropolitans on the grand prince. This is also disclosed in the ecclesiastical architecture in Moscow: the Cathedral of the Assumption of Mary with the burial places of the grand princes and the Cathedral of the Archangel not only have religious significance but also express a political message. This is evident in the full title of the head of the church: the title "Metropolitan of Kiev" was expanded to "and of the Entire Rus'."

The Missionary Work of the Russian Church

In a narrower sense, the acquisition of principalities and the concentration of power in Moscow belong to the "gathering of the Russian land." In a broader sense, it also means the process of annexing territory in the north and in the east. There are various reasons for this process, and it occurred in various ways: the cultivation of the claimed land during which a forest was cleared and cultivated only for a few years, and then another forest was used; the advance of monks who, in their search for solitude, pushed farther into the unknown wilderness; and the deliberate, active mission among non-Christian peoples. The first way is significant for the church in that it expanded Christianity on and on, away from population centers and known territories. In the other two ways, the ecclesiastical significance is quite obvious.

The opening up of space by monks is important. It is anchored in the idea that one must leave the "world," and it recalls the beginning of Christian monasticism in Egypt, Palestine, and Syria. In Russia, this process becomes apparent in the increasing replacement of urban monasteries by hermitages. Monks withdrew alone, or with one disciple, into the wilderness of a forest, established a cell and a chapel, and were self-sufficient. In time, new monasteries originated at these locations because the hermitage became known and attracted more young men who wanted to become disciples of the hermit. Settlements originated around the monasteries. The process repeated itself; individual monks wanted to live as hermits and moved on in order to establish a new hermitage. This process ensured that, above all, in the territories north of the upper Volga whole tracts of land were cleared for cultivation. This is also shown by the fact that there were, and still are, a series of monasteries that are distanced from each other by a day's journey. From 1429 until 1436, the famous Solovetskiy Monastery was built on an island in the White Sea at the uttermost north of the country; it was to acquire great wealth in the future.

The figure of the Starets is to be seen in the background, the wise monk with a model personality that will be described later. Here, as always in the history of monasticism, a phenomenon is to be noted, namely, that these monasteries became greater and greater and well-to-do in time, which raises the question of the original principles. Moreover, the monasteries represented a threat to the grand prince through their economic weight. Consequently, the rulers made repeated attempts to control church property (and that meant, above all, monastic property).

Besides the monastic colonization, there also was the deliberate and systematic mission with the goal to proclaim the gospel to non-Christian peoples and to spread Christianity in this manner. Although it did not have to be, it was frequently connected with the conquest of the territory in question through the Russian state and was not infrequently carried out with great force. But beyond that, missions were also established outside the borders of the empire, above all, in Asia (China since 1700, Japan since 1870, Korea since 1897).

One of the first Russian missionaries was Bishop Stefan of Perm

(d. 1396), who did successful work among the Zyrians, a Finno-Ugric tribe in the north of the country (today Komi). He learned to speak their language, created an alphabet for it, and translated numerous works and writings into their language. But reports from subsequent centuries show that this and most of the other missionary enterprises did not endure. Again and again, complaints could be heard about reconversions to the original religion (above all, among Muslims), and there were reports from those who remained Orthodox that pagan superstitions and pre-Christian practices survived.

The mission to the east was quite systematically pursued. Very early, after the fifteenth century, Siberia was regarded as a territory to be conquered and Christianized. The acquisition of Siberia happened, in part, militarily, but also frequently through merchants who brought with them, above all, animal skins and precious metals. They were accompanied by missionaries who stayed in the emerging fortified locations. The priests were occupied with the spiritual care for Russians now living in Siberia as well as with the mission to the "pagans," who were mostly followers of shamanism or animism.

After the eighteenth century, the Russian Church established dioceses in Siberia to augment the diocese of Tobolsk, founded in 1620, which had been long responsible for the entire region. Filofey of Tobolsk made missionary trips also to China and altogether founded thirty-seven churches before his death in 1727. The missionaries paid special attention to the translation of the most significant books of Christianity into the respective languages. Thus it was necessary to be devoted to language study; many languages received their first grammar and writing in this manner. Later, budding missionaries were trained, above all, at the academy of Kazan in Asiatic languages. After the eighteenth century, stations for mission were established in Siberia so that missionaries were present permanently in a region, and not only when they were there for commercial purposes.

The first mission to Alaska in 1793 was a great and important step. The "Apostle of Alaska," the monk German (or Herman), was active there until his death in 1837. In 1840, a bishopric was founded for the Kamchatka Peninsula; the bishopric was also responsible for America. The mission proceeded via Russian Alaska southward along the western coast of America as far as California, where there are still today a few Russian churches from that time. That is why the first ecclesiastical presence of Russian Orthodoxy in North America is not due to migration (via western Europe and the eastern coast of America) but to the mission from the north. In 1870, a bishopric was established and soon transferred to San Francisco. Only the sale of Alaska to the United States in 1867 gradually ended these missionary efforts because San Francisco was too far away from missionary territories. The number of Russian immigrants to the USA grew, and the residence of the bishop was moved to New York in 1905. The still existing Orthodox Church of America, which, however, is not canonically acknowledged by all Orthodox churches, is partly the result of these missionary efforts.

In 1870, Bishop Innokentiy (Popov-Venyaminov) of the Aleutian Islands founded the Russian Missionary Society when he was metropolitan of Moscow. Orthodox missionaries also arrived in Japan from the east. In 1862, Bishop Nikolay (Kasatkin), honored later as the father of Japanese Orthodoxy, created as a young monk the foundation for the still existing Japanese Orthodox Church, first at the consular church in Hokkaido, then through organized missionary work. He became bishop in 1880 and archbishop in 1906, and made an early effort for the inculturation of Orthodoxy in Japan. The Japanese Orthodox Church was assigned an autocephalous status by Russian Orthodoxy in 1970. But the other Orthodox churches did not acknowledge it.

Finally, the missionary work among the members of the Assyrian Church in the Persian Empire needs to be mentioned. A larger group of them joined the Russian Church in 1898.

The foreign missions are an indirect result of the Russian conquests in the Far East. They are to be viewed in connection with the expansion of the empire. The case is different with regard to Muslims who have lived in significant numbers in Russia since the sixteenth century (conquest of Kazan). The Russian state first tried to convert the Muslims of mostly Turkish descent through material stimulations in the south and the southeast of the empire. Baptized Muslims were exempt from the poll tax. Occasionally, they received cash and were spared from recruiting. Obviously, there were also numerous forced baptisms. Occasionally, administrative measures appeared, such as the prohibition of mosques. Nevertheless, the missionary successes among Muslims remained very poor. Many of them returned to Islam. The toleration, manifested under Catherine II and later in the legislation after 1905, made it still more difficult for the Orthodox Church to attain missionary successes among Muslims. On the other hand, there hardly was a mission among Jews who lived in the western territories after the acquisitions of the seventeenth and eighteenth centuries.

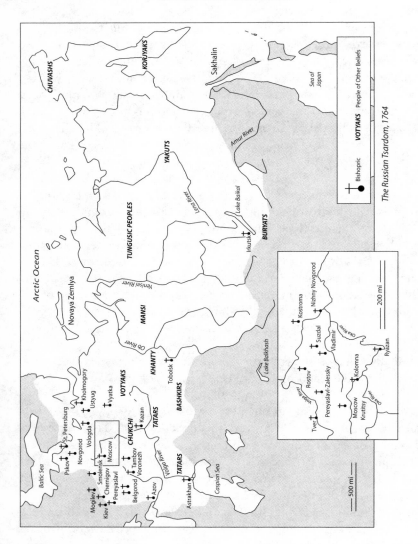

The Russian Tsardom, 1764

They were discriminated against, especially through prohibitions of settlement. Individual conversions were accepted, but there was no organized missionary effort among the Jewish population. The members of churches in union with Rome in these territories were frequently not compelled by the authorities to become Orthodox after their church was prohibited; they were urged to join the Roman Catholic Church.

So the missionary work of the Russian Church is conditioned to a great extent by the expansion of the Moscow and later the Russian empire. The mission related to "paganism," that is, above all, with the members of traditional religions. The intensity of the mission was strongly dependent on political circumstances. In Siberia, the government of the tsar also usually prohibited missionary efforts by missionaries of other Christian churches, for example, by Jesuits, or by the Community of the Moravian Brethren. Conversion to Christianity always meant conversion to Orthodoxy.

As a rule, mission was also linked with being Russian. That meant, above all, that ecclesiastical Church Slavonic was introduced as liturgical language (whereby the principle of Orthodoxy was often violated to celebrate the liturgy in the native language). The translation of important writings into the respective languages did, of course, often determine those languages' origin or codification. Moreover, regulations mandated the translation of the confession of faith before baptism and other central Christian texts into the respective languages. Russian often gained the upper hand, however, because it was the official language and *lingua franca* in the Russian Empire (and is still today often used in the successor states). Consequently, missionary work was not only a religious process but also always a cultural one. Despite the numerous regulations that the customs of converted tribes be respected, only a consciousness of belonging to a specific nation has frequently remained until today; it has no other forms of expression. The Soviet regime, in particular, saw to it that, in its claim to not only create justice for classes but also to bring freedom to peoples oppressed in the empire of the tsar, the languages of peoples in the republics and of national minorities were promoted. But the example of Russification of Orthodoxy in Georgia shows how often the acceptance of central elements of Russian culture was connected with the adoption of Christianity.

In recent years, there has been a sporadic recognition of the need for a theology of mission for the present. Here, a change of perspective occurred: mission is no longer directed to the outside but is basically related to a society that has already been opened for Christianity. In this sense, the needs of the church in a post-Soviet society are to be met. But such efforts are still in the early stages.

Emigration and Schisms

Russian Orthodoxy not only expanded wherever Russia was, but it was also present in foreign countries that lacked a traditional Orthodoxy. Here, the dynastic relations of the house of the tsars, above all with German nobility, played an increasing role after the eighteenth century. In the nineteenth century, Germany (besides France) was a popular country for the traveling Russian nobility. This is evidenced not only by German words in Russian, such as *kurort* for "spa" or *buterbrod* for "sandwich," but also by church buildings in spas: in Baden-Baden, Bad Homburg, Bad Ems, and Wiesbaden, Russian churches and chapels from that time are still admired today.

The greatest expansion of Russian Orthodoxy in the West occurred in the twentieth century as a consequence of the Russian Revolution. During the civil war, numerous bishops stayed in territories occupied by the "Whites," whom they also supported politically. But when the Red Army advanced and the "Whites" retreated, they, too, were compelled to leave the country. This happened mostly by ship via the Black Sea to Constantinople, then on to other European countries. The emigration concentrated first on the two monarchies with Slavic languages, namely, Yugoslavia and Bulgaria, as well as Poland, Germany, and France. In 1921, a Russian synod was established in Sremski Karlovci (Yugoslavia), a place of great significance for Serbian Orthodoxy, under the earlier Kiev metropolitan Antoniy (Khrapovitskiy). Members of the synod appealed to a decree of Patriarch Tikhon (Belavin) from 1920, demanding the organization of bishops on their own without contacting the patriarch. This synod, later called "the synod of Karlovtsi," called for the overthrow of the Bolsheviks and the restoration of the monarchy in Russia. Patriarch Tikhon tried to undo the synod and transfer the leadership of the Russian Church abroad to the moderate metropolitan of Paris, Yevlogiy (Georgiyevskiy). Yevlogiy obeyed and, in the face of the situation in the Soviet Union in 1931, put Russian Orthodoxy in France under the authority of the Ecumenical Patriarch of Constantinople as well as the Russian Church in the USA. But the synod in Yugoslavia did not acknowledge the decision of Tikhon because it had been made under the pressure of the government. After a declaration of loyalty to the Soviet state by the Moscow metropolitan Sergiy (Stragorodskiy) in 1927, the synod finally separated from the church in the mother country.

During the Yugoslavian exile between the two wars, the church succeeded to consolidate abroad. Russian nuns contributed to the revival of feminine monasticism in the Serbian church, and a seminary was established for the training of priests. Publications of the church could appear, and many Russian theologians participated substantially in the origin and development of the theological faculty in Belgrade. During the disturbances of World War II, the synod transferred its residence first, for a brief time, to Carlsbad (Karlovy Vary) and Munich, and established a center in the USA in 1950, where it called itself the Russian Orthodox Church Abroad, claiming to be the only free part of Russian Orthodoxy. During the Soviet period, there were no connections with the patriarchal church in Moscow. The church abroad viewed the patriarchy as being in bondage and represented a sharp anti-Communist stance.

The church abroad was represented, above all, in the classic countries of emigration in western Europe, in North America, in Latin America, as well as in Australia. It endured several schisms and crises, and it represented the majority of the Russian emigration community. In 1981, its conservative-national disposition was disclosed when it canonized the last tsar, Nikolay II, who was killed, together with his family, by the Bolsheviks.

It was a problem for the patriarchal church that the church abroad denounced the persecution of religion in the Soviet Union; it was also supported in its stance by the West. The church in Moscow knew that these reproaches were right but was silent about them because it existed, of course, in the country and did not want to endanger its weak position. Supported by government authorities, it also established parishes abroad, sending priests and bishops there so that the church of the Moscow patriarchy was present everywhere, and a network of Russian dioceses originated abroad. But these parishes almost never had the number of members of the church abroad. In the USA and in Japan, the Orthodox churches in communion with Moscow were made autocephalous. But this action was not acknowledged by Orthodoxy as a whole, and the canonical status of both churches is still unclear today.

The church abroad lost its legitimate basis after the end of the religious persecution in Russia and the collapse of the Soviet Union. The patriarchal church was now no longer in bondage. First, the church abroad tried to identify and make contact with catacomb churches that survived the Soviet period. Some dioceses were founded in Russia and in the CIS (Commonwealth of Independent States). Later, it established contact with conservative, above all, antiecumenical, circles within the patriarchal church, and, finally, it established official relations with the head of the patriarchy. The ROC, in its turn, showed great interest in reunification, and open questions were cleared in several rounds of dialogue. In May 2007 the unification of both churches was solemnly celebrated.

It is not easy to describe the present state of the church abroad, which has a half-autonomous status within the ROC after the reunification. It has nine dioceses and about 450 parishes worldwide. The number of believers cannot be precisely determined since it apparently has substantially decreased in recent years. The contacts with the Moscow Church led to a great crisis because not all its members approved such relations. Moreover, a conflict within the leadership of the church intensified the situation.

The number of Orthodox Russians in western countries has again strongly increased after the descendants of the "classic" emigrants of the first wave (after the October Revolution) and of the second wave (in connection with World War II) have more and more assimilated. There are several reasons for this new phenomenon: the possibility to emigrate for Soviet Jews and for Russian Germans with their occasional Orthodox family members, as well as the migrations after the end of the Soviet Union. The worship services of the Russian parishes in Germany are ordinarily well attended, and Orthodoxy in Germany today is, not the least through Russian Christians, the third-largest church with more than a million believers.

A phenomenon, indirectly related to this, needs to be mentioned in connection with the expansion of Russian Orthodoxy in the twentieth century: a few years after the revolution, numerous intellectuals, known as religious thinkers, were exiled. Among them was the theologian Sergiy Bulgakov, who went to Paris and there became the rector of the newly established Saint-Serge Orthodox Theological Institute. In 1938, still before the war, a similar institution originated in New York, St. Vladimir's Seminary. Both contributed in great measure to a fruitful exchange between Orthodox and Western theology. Meanwhile, there are a number of scientific theological establishments in the West. But these two Russian institutes must be named first.

Today, the ROC of the Moscow patriarchate is present worldwide. Among its total of 223 dioceses, 99 are abroad (45 in Ukraine, 34 in other successor states of the USSR, 3 in Japan, 9 in the "ROC outside Russia," and 8 in the "far abroad," i.e., western Europe and South America).[9] It sets value on founding parishes in the West for the care of its believers but not for mission. In the meantime, however, a great number of Catholics and Protestants have converted to Orthodoxy. In some parishes, worship services are conducted in the respective language of the country. The church claims to be present everywhere in Russia and, beyond that, wherever there are Orthodox Russians.

9. The church does not indicate the number of believers, but only the number of dioceses, monasteries, and parishes.

CHAPTER FOUR

Ecclesiastical Structures

The survey of the epoch of Russian church history showed that the structure of Russian Orthodoxy, its constitution, and its canonical affiliation have repeatedly changed. The question of ecclesiastical structure not only includes organizational character but also impacts the inner condition of a church, as well as its possibilities to act outside, above all, in relation to the state. The history of Russian Orthodoxy indicates that the conditions for the framework, set by Orthodox ecclesiology, were often very extensively interpreted.

The Juridical Dependence on Constantinople

After its establishment, the metropolis of Kiev remained, for the time being, dependent on Constantinople. This was in accord with the principle that the imperial capital was responsible for the bishops "among the barbarians." Other patriarchies could not be considered anyway. Any independence of the Russian Church would have been inconceivable from the very start because a mission church remained, for the time being, in juridical dependence. That is why an ecclesiastical province was created, led by the Kiev metropolitan. He was appointed in Constantinople, or at least confirmed there. But bishops under his authority were elected at their sees by the respective princes, or by representatives of the people (as in Novgorod). There is the well-known case of a bishop, a Greek, who had been nominated by the metropolitan but was rejected because he had not been elected by the "people of our land." If contact with Constantinople was not possible, or the patriarchal throne was vacant, a successor of the metropolitan was nominated by the grand prince and, as far as possible, confirmed later. The renowned metropolitan Ilarion, the first attested Slav in this function, obtained his office in this way in 1051, since it was not possible to confirm him at the time because of a war. So the consciousness predominated that basically the approval of the imperial city had to be sought. But in concrete situations of exceptions, other solutions were also possible.

Little is known about the beginnings of the ecclesiastical organization. To be sure, two names of metropolitans are known, but an occupant of this office is certain only for the year 1039, named Feopempt (Theopemptos). In the early period, to be sure, Greeks and Slavs took turns occupying the chair of the metropolitan. But later, there were more and more "Russians." However, the last metropolitan, nominated by Constantinople in the fifteenth century, was a Greek.

There is also little information about suffragan bishops. In 1036, Grand Prince Yaroslav the Wise appointed a bishop in Novgorod, the second most important city. It is remarkable that this appointment did not happen through an ecclesiastical authority, such as the patriarch or the metropolitan; it happened through the secular ruler. Gradually, the other cities in the principalities also received bishops who, however, were almost always Slavs. In the eleventh century, altogether nine dioceses were established in the Rus'. In the middle of the twelfth century, there were twelve dioceses (including Kiev).

A difficult situation arose in the ecclesiastical structure when a second metropolis originated in Kiev after the destruction of the city and the beginning of the shift of the center of gravity to the north to Vladimir. The departure of the metropolitan had created a vacuum in old Kiev. The princes of neighboring Halich in the west were interested in the city and the residence of a metropolitan there. They also had developed their own Western foreign policy and had made contacts with Rome after the center of power of the Rus' had moved to the north. That is why their efforts for Kiev proceeded not without any exercise of Roman influence. Lithuania, which had become a great power, though still pagan, was also interested in the Kiev see and, of course, in the patriarchy in Constantinople. Here, one strove for an indirect influence of Lithuania since the weight of the Roman Church increased there. The name "Little Russia" appeared for this territory, as seen from Constantinople, because this Rus' could be reached in a brief journey in contrast to the more distant Rus' in the north, "Great Russia."

In the fourteenth century, an ecclesiastical province was finally established in Kiev after long discussions and changing relations of power, and after Lviv and Halich had fallen to Poland. Thus both locations came permanently under the influence of the West. Lviv, today in western Ukraine, received the municipal law of Magdeburg and developed, in many respects, analogous to other western European cities. The differences between the west and the east of Ukraine, still existing today, originate in this basic, twofold development: Lviv and Galicia under western European influence, the eastern part of the land marked by the Orthodox tradition. Later developments, such as the Habsburg period in Galicia, contributed still more in strengthening this difference.

Now there were two metropolitanates of Kiev, one in the city and one transferred to Vladimir, that is, Moscow. After the transaction of the first Polish-Lithuanian union, which lasted from 1386 until 1492, the Lithuanian dynasty became Catholic. Since many principalities of the old Rus' belonged to this commonwealth, Orthodox believers represented the majority of the population there. But they fell into an uncomfortable situation because the rulers favored the Roman Catholic Church. The see of the metropolitan of Kiev had to remain vacant again and again, since Constantinople was too weak to intervene decisively in this question. The see was permanently occupied only in the fifteenth century, and then by Orthodox metropolitans who acknowledged the patriarch of Constantinople. Since the Russian Church declared itself independent of Constantinople at the same time, and the metropolitan changed his title to "of Moscow and the whole Rus'," the problem of a double metropolis no longer existed. Kiev had lost its significance for Russian Orthodoxy. When the union between Poland and Lithuania was renewed in 1569, the city fell to Poland. The Union of Brest in 1596 caused further unrest in the Orthodox Church of the region. The Polish state now acknowledged only those hierarchies that declared their allegiance to the union with Rome. After 1620, there was again an Orthodox metropolitan in Kiev. When the eastern Ukraine on the left of the river and the city of Kiev finally fell to Russia in 1667, Kiev remained, for the time being, a simple diocese. Soon thereafter, in 1685, it was revalued again as a metropolitanate within the Russian patriarchy.

These events point to several aspects: First, Kiev had no real enduring significance for the Russian Church except as the city of Christianization and of the rise of the Rus'. Undoubtedly, a transfer of power and of ecclesiastical authority had occurred in the Russian consciousness. The title of Kiev was still claimed in the fifteenth century. But the independence of Russian Orthodoxy made it an ecclesiastical association of its own in which the name Kiev did not even play a role anymore. Only at the end of the seventeenth century did Kiev again return to the collective memory of Russian Orthodoxy.

Second, the Roman See made repeated attempts to influence Kiev. Now, the state belonged to the Catholic world because of the Christianization of Lithuania, and Rome's realm of influence had shifted significantly to the east. This influence became greater through the increase of the power of Lithuania. It had made arrangements with the Teutonic Order, which ruled over many Slavic principalities, and had access to the Black Sea. Consequently, claims were often openly expressed, indicated by the fact that the Lithuanian bishops (in misjudgment of the real circumstances) were appointed as vicar-generals for all of Russia. That is why there were repeated attempts to appoint Catholic bishops in Kiev, first, those of the Latin rite, then, after the Union of Florence in 1439, those who were "Uniate."

Thus, the special nature of two Kiev ecclesiastical traditions is disclosed, both appealing to the Christianization under Vladimir. This development must also be viewed on the background of the Tartar invasion that had caused the development of several centers of the Rus'. Both Kiev traditions share the disagreement with the West (with different results) as well as the Greek heritage. The tradition in Russia can be considered unbroken, but the location changed and, finally, so did the name. The Kiev tradition stayed in Kiev, but with several interruptions in continuity, as well as in ecclesiastical and national affiliation. In the twentieth century, the different interpretations of these developments were to still provide much material for conflict.

Autocephaly and Patriarchy

The autocephaly of the Russian Church is an indirect consequence of the Council of Ferrara-Florence where the Church of Constantinople entered into a union with the Roman Church in 1439, hoping, in this way, to receive military assistance against the Ottomans, who pressed hard against the empire. The principle of this union required Eastern Christians to acknowledge the Roman primacy and declare the Latin convictions to be correct, but it also allowed them to keep, in return, their own customs and traditions. The union did not last long. Metropolitan Isidore, one of its main advocates, who was responsible for Russia, tried to introduce it in Moscow, but he was unsuccessful and saved himself only by fleeing. Consequently, Bishop Iona, who had been passed over earlier, was appointed metropolitan in Moscow without any consultation with Constantinople (which, of course, in Russian eyes had renounced the faith, as Isidore did through the union). Thus, the Moscow Church was de facto autocephalous, that is, no longer dependent on any other jurisdiction, and could henceforth appoint its own leaders. A logical conclusion was the renaming, the Metropolis of Moscow and of the Entire Rus', because the title "of Kiev" had always also implied the subordination under Constantinople. This action was confirmed at a Moscow synod in 1459, after the fall of Constantinople. The ecumenical patriarchy, however, only acknowledged the Moscow autocephaly considerably later. For this reason, the Russian Church was isolated in Orthodoxy. In 1458, Rome appointed a friend of the union, a monk named Gregorios from Constantinople, as metropolitan of Kiev, Halich, and All of Russia. But in Moscow no value was set any longer on the title of Kiev. The separation of the two church bodies was accomplished.

The autocephaly of the church of Moscow had far-reaching consequences, even though the administration of the church already existed, in great measure, independent of the ecumenical patriarchy. The Russian Church was now no longer obliged to be subject to the former imperial city in ecclesiastical affairs. The decisions made there by the synod were valid for all metropolitanates and thus also for the one in Kiev. The Orthodox Church in the Moscow empire could now arrange its internal affairs on its own. The election of the metropolitan certainly was the point at which this became most evident. Outside relations were left to the state alone, since the borders between the state and ecclesiastical jurisdiction were in agreement. Subsequently, Metropolitan Feodosiy, the successor of Metropolitan Iona, took the title "of Moscow and the Entire Rus'" when he came into office in 1461. "Rus'" no longer counted as the historical structure, consisting of the principalities of the Rus', but now as the territory under the rule of the Moscow empire. Only later, reference was made again to the historical notion, not without imperial intentions.

The isolation of the Russian Church within the total church, based on its own declaration of autocephaly, meant, first of all, difficult or interrupted relations with the rest of Orthodoxy, especially since all other churches existed in the Ottoman Empire (not counting the Orthodox churches in Poland-Lithuania). Only Russia was an Orthodox state not ruled by foreigners. Soon, this was to become obvious in the financial dependence of eastern patriarchies on Moscow. There were also only sporadic contacts with the Western church. The union was already understood as a hostile act, and the continuing attempts of the Catholic neighbors Poland and Lithuania to gain a foothold in Moscow did not contribute to improved relations. This isolation, which was not only related to the church in the fifteenth and sixteenth centuries, caused influences from the outside to reach Moscow generally later, which then also frequently encountered rejection.

The contested meaning of the idea of Moscow as the "third Rome" is evidence of this rejection. Accordingly, the downfall of Constantinople is understood as God's punishment for the union with the Roman heretics. Moscow is, after Rome and Constantinople, the "new Rome," the third Rome, "because two Romes have fallen, and a third stands, and a fourth there not shall be," as was written by the monk Filofey in the early sixteenth century.[1] Even though the text and this notion did not endure, they still show how much the Moscow empire was understood as successor of the Byzantine Empire, together with the Russian Church as the church at large.

Ecclesiastical independence was complete when the church was elevated to a patriarchy. To be analogous to Byzantium meant to have also a patriarch as head of the church besides the Orthodox emperor. When in the "time of troubles," in the uncertainties of dynastic succession of Ivan IV ("the "Terrible") after 1589, an ecumenical patriarch stayed, for the first time, in Moscow, Boris Godunov negotiated as the regent with him about the elevation of the Moscow Church to the patriarchy. The financial situation of Orthodoxy in the Ottoman Empire forced representatives of these churches again and again to beg for support in Moscow. That reduced it to a state of dependency on the tsar, who was quite aware of it. After negotiations with Jeremiah II, he agreed to elevate the metropolitan to "Patriarch of Moscow and of the Entire Rus' and the Northern Territories." His successors were to be elected "for eternal times" by Russian synods. The result was not damaged because the negotiations were

---

1. Quoted after Marshall Poe, "Moscow, the Third Rome: The Origins and Transformations of a 'Pivotal Moment,'" *Jahrbücher für die Geschichte Osteuropas* 49 (2001): 412-29, here 416.

conducted by the sovereign and not the church. But it demonstrates the significance of the elevation to the patriarchy for the Moscow empire. The decision was confirmed at several synods in Constantinople and also by the remaining patriarchs or their deputies. In this manner, the Russian Church was again incorporated into all of Orthodoxy. The isolation was breached, resulting in a renewed rapprochement with Greek Christianity that would also show itself in increased influence in theology, ecclesiastical art, and church administration.

Thus, a patriarchate had been established, for the first time, in modern times. The traditional sequence of patriarchates, customary since antiquity — Constantinople, Alexandria, Antioch, and Jerusalem — had now been supplemented by a fifth, that is, Moscow. The Russian patriarch was obliged to view the see of Constantinople as the first, "as do also all other patriarchs." The independence of the church was now complete in every respect. The term "autocrat" was finally adopted in the title of the tsars: an autocrat like the Byzantine emperor who, in his dominion, would not have to be dependent on, established by, or confirmed by anyone on earth. The continuity of Byzantium, which had also become evident in taking possession of elements of protocol, became evident again here. Patriarch Jeremiah II also had committed Moscow and its church to defend the Greek faith, a task of Russia as protecting power opposite to the Muslims who, above all, in subsequent centuries were to gain greater significance.

The attainment of the patriarchy also implied a reorganization of the church from within. Four new metropolitanates were created, as were six new archbishoprics and three new dioceses (besides the five old ones). In subsequent years more dioceses were founded, above all in the northern and eastern territories. However, the elevation of the patriarchate did not change significantly its relatively weak position opposite the rulers. In the sixteenth century alone, five of the eleven Moscow metropolitans were dismissed. This was no longer that simple when patriarchs were concerned (even though it happened once). But the rulers viewed the church as part of the state and, therefore, as subjugated to their authority, so one can speak de facto of a dominion of the tsar over the church. The occasionally successful attempts of some metropolitans and patriarchs to become more independent do not change this situation.

The Russian Church used its independence also to stabilize its faith and piety. The Hundred-Chapter Synod (*stoglav* in Russian) of 1551 introduced numerous reforms, especially in the realm of liturgy. Many abuses had crept in over time. Certainly, the best known of them was "parallel singing" *(mnogoglasiye)*. Several choirs sang simultaneously various parts of the liturgy in order to shorten the long worship services. This and other deviations were stopped. It was agreed to use uniform patterns in the painting of icons. The jurisdiction of eparchies (dioceses) and the supervision of the clergy were strengthened, and also monastic discipline. The reforms rejected everything that was perceived as "strange" and confirmed most of the Russian special developments. The attempt of the tsar to secularize monastic property was largely thwarted. Barely a century after the Hundred-Chapter Synod, in 1649, the "Nomo-Canon" was printed, a collection of decisions of the Eastern canon law; this was a sign of the need for a constitution with rules for life in the church. In the same year, the conflict between the liturgical reformers and their critics ignited for the first time. It was to lead to the schism of the Old Believers. Finally, the Great Moscow Council of 1666-67, assembled in connection with these disputes, decided to improve the liturgical rites and confirmed the independence of the patriarch in ecclesiastical affairs. But de facto, the rulers could impose their will on the church.

Events in foreign policy affected the church insofar as there now existed Orthodox Christianity west of the Moscow empire through the extension of Lithuania to the east and the failure of the union of the fifteenth century. The Moscow metropolitans and patriarchs regarded the Orthodox in Poland-Lithuania as part of their jurisdiction. Here, however, there was little room for negotiations, and even less after the Union of Brest with its consequences. When the eastern Ukraine and Kiev became part of Russia, only one part of this problem was solved. According to the Russian version, this development was understood as "reunification" of Ukraine with Russia, but in the Ukrainian version it was thought of as another period of bondage, this time under Russian rule.

The Synodical Phase

The ecclesiastical reforms, ordered by Tsar Peter I at the beginning of the eighteenth century, were the most extensive ones in the time of the tsars. They changed the external shape of the church, especially its leadership, for centuries and brought it still more under the control of the state. Above all, they were based on theological presuppositions that were not derived from the Orthodox tradition. To that extent, these reforms can be considered under the aspect of ecclesiastical structure, as well as in regard to the relation of state and church, or also in the context of the history of theology, shaped by the Western influence. The reforms did not come out of nothing. They disclose Western influences from the previous years. Already in 1687, a "Slavic-Greek-Latin School" had been founded. Intensive debates about the introduction of Latin had preceded this foundation whose beginnings can be traced back to the reign of Tsar Fyodor (1676-82). Thus it becomes evident that Western influences, against which the church tried to defend itself, had already been received before Peter.

The idea of modernizing the political system according to the Western model was the background of Peter's reforms. The state was to serve the "common good," as it was said again and again. Many elements of the Russian Church hampered this process, such as the disputes with the Old Believers that Peter had inherited, and the cumbersome, old-fashioned, and anti-Western patriarchal church. So these elements themselves became the object of Peter's politics of reform. The most important innovations within the church were the abolition of the patriarchal office and the establishment of a synod as the governing agency in the church, the restriction of monastic life, and measures for improving the education of the clergy.

The last two patriarchs, Ioakim and Adrian, had been clearly aware of the need of the church to be strong. They continued the course of Patriarch Nikon, who already had followed it against the Old Believers (but, in the final analysis, did not succeed). This was not a simple situation for the young Tsar Peter who could begin his reign only after family quarrels and rivalries. When Adrian died in 1700, Peter permitted no new election but placed Bishop Stefan Yavorskiy as administrator of the patriarchal office. Yavorskiy came from Lviv and had been educated in philosophy and theology at Polish Jesuit schools; that is, he had been a Catholic in the early phase of his life. Later he went to Kiev as a teacher of theology and as abbot. Peter brought him from there to Russia. On the basis of his origin, he can be considered a representative of the Latinizing trend of Ukrainian Orthodoxy, evidenced by his use of Catholic arguments when faced with Protestant views, such as the priority of tradition over Scripture. Nevertheless, he remained strictly Orthodox so that he was critical also of Peter's reforms. In the final analysis, the tsar had his will; Yavorskiy even later became the first president of the synod.

Peter had to reckon with opposition from the church in his reforms.

But he could keep it under control with the help of the administrator of the synod as well as through administrative measures. Opposition had to be expected, above all, from the conservative circles of the church and from monasticism. That is why the significance of this factor had to be largely excluded.

In 1701, a new Monastic Office was established to exercise authority over monastic property — one more link in the long chain of attempts by the state to acquire the monastic property. Even though this was not yet completely achieved (the office was again dissolved in 1720), some restrictions succeeded. The state relinquished neither its claim to hold ecclesiastical property at its disposal, nor its other pressures against the church. Many monasteries were dissolved. Entrance to them was made quite difficult; for men only after thirty, for women after sixty. The tsar wanted to prevent able-bodied people doing "useless" work rather than serving the common good. The remaining monasteries were urged to dedicate themselves to "useful" activities, that is, to works of charity.

After 1718, Peter became more fully occupied with the organization of the church. The metropolitan of Petersburg, Feofan Prokopovich, became his most important adviser. He also came from Ukraine and had been temporarily a Catholic, having studied in Rome where he had come to know Jesuit theology. After his return, he became abbot of the Cave Monastery in Kiev and, in 1716, metropolitan of the new capital. His theological orientation has been described as influenced by Protestantism, disclosed in the adoption of some Protestant principles, such as the primacy of Scripture and the doctrine of justification. On the whole, he was able to defend Orthodox principles against reproaches because of his knowledge of Western theology, above all, its method. Since many Russian theologians were to proceed that way in the future, he is considered the "father of Russian theology." The fact that this method also encountered sharp criticism will be the subject in chapter 6, dealing with theology and religious thought.

Prokopovich had a positive attitude toward reforms. He published *The Right of the Will of the Monarch,* which described the tsar as the supreme shepherd and hierarch. Accordingly, the will of the people was manifested in the will of the monarch. Here, one can find Byzantine conceptions as well as Russian ideas and reminiscences of the Western doctrine of natural law. In 1721, Prokopovich wrote the programmatic *Spiritual Regulation.* It tried to present a total reorientation of the Russian Church. Western conceptions and principles are clearly adopted in this statute. The synod is introduced with a rationale (a group has more advantages than an individual) as a collective governing body of the church; the single jurisdiction of the bishop no longer plays a decisive role. We must recall that, on the one hand, the tsar knew of the principle of a synodical, nonmonarchical government in western Europe, and that, on the other hand, the church was structured parallel to the other public institutions. The church became part of the state, just like the ministries or the senate. It was no longer an independent corporate body within the state. Such attitudes could still be frequently encountered later in nations affected by Orthodoxy.

In 1721, the Most Holy Governing Synod constituted itself as the "Spiritual Collegium," analogous to the other *collegia* (ministries) Peter had introduced. Soon it was renamed and had to be also commemorated in the liturgy at the place where prayers were offered for the patriarch. First, there was one president of the synod; the office was entrusted to Yavorskiy, who, as an opponent of the reforms, now occupied a responsible position. After his death in 1722, the office remained vacant, and the public officer in the governing body with the title chief procurator became more and more significant. Peter himself and tsars after him frequently influenced the activities of the synod.

The establishment of the synod institutionalized a tension between the spiritual government of the church, which remained with the bishops because of their power to ordain, and the de facto church government, which had been transferred to the synod. There were two consequences. (1) The importance and esteem of the bishops subsided strongly with regard to spirituality; instead, the role of the monks became more important since they represented for many people, above all in the nineteenth century, the spiritual authority par excellence. (2) The guidance of the church switched de facto to the chief procurator. This development culminated under Konstantin Pobedonostsev, who held office from 1880 to 1905. He exercised a strong control over the church, which he viewed as a pillar of the autocracy. The supervision of schools was transferred to the church, and the bishops were also to control the monks and the Startsy; but this did not prove possible. Although the chief procurators had no right to vote, they were present at all sessions, they kept in contact with the tsar, and they controlled all correspondence of the synod and the bishops. Consequently, all measures and activities of the bishops were dependent on the synod to a high degree.

The measures of Peter also had consequences for the education of the clergy. His enlightened mind favored a good education of the priests. Education was basically considered an important task of the church, again in the background of the ideal conception of the common good. To it belonged the obligatory establishment of theological schools in the dioceses so that the education standard of the priests could be elevated. This could, of course, not be achieved everywhere, but it did represent a basis for the improvement of clerical education. Even though a comprehensive educational system could not be created quickly, the attempt was made to influence the common good through the priests; they were to provide instruction, above all, in sermons. This was the background for, among other things, the establishment of the Moscow Theological Academy, which, however, under Yavorskiy strove first rather for a Latinizing education. Prokopovich founded a boarding school in Petersburg as a rival institution where, above all, secular subjects were taught. This also corresponded with the desire of the tsar, who wanted clergymen to be fit not only for the church but also for other functions in the state, for the common good.

The two most important theologians of the time were rivals of each other while vicariously affirming their theological tendencies. With all necessary limitation of generalizations, Yavorskiy was an exponent of a rather Catholic tendency while Prokopovich was one of a rather Protestant one. This is to be traced, above all, to their theological education and development. It is symptomatic for the Russian Church and theology of the time, which had sharply differentiated itself for a long time from all Western influences, that the extensive reorientations had been introduced by theologians who represented Western tendencies. One's own tradition might perhaps have offered resistance to Peter's reforms, but it could not have offered a sound alternative model. Nevertheless, the situation may not be understood as if Yavorskiy and Prokopovich had not been unambiguously Orthodox. They both agreed in their rejection of the Western churches (by the way, also of the Greeks) and remained firm Orthodox hierarchs. They were not aware of "early ecumenical" ideas, and they plainly rejected endeavors for union, already known to them from their Ukrainian homeland, as machinations of the Roman Church. Even though many bishops and theologians were to be called in the coming decades from Ukraine to dioceses in Russia, above all Siberia, or to functions in the government of the church, the church still remained clearly Orthodox. There even were proceedings against openly Protestant, above all pietist, or Catholic, tendencies. Tsar Peter also never questioned the orthodoxy of the church.

The reforms of Peter are still today quite differently interpreted. Peter is frequently presented as a counterpart to Ivan IV. It is said that Ivan had preserved Russian values, resisted all Western influences with loyalty and strength to Orthodoxy, and showed Russians that they had a future only by appealing to their own traditions and by remaining united. But Peter had opened Russia to pernicious Western influences; alien values had become more important than their own traditions, and all misfortune that Russia had to fight against in the time to come came from there. The dispute between both positions found expression, above all, in the Russian philosophy of the nineteenth century when the "Slavophiles" and the "Westernizers" faced each other, and it was revived again after the collapse of the Soviet Union.

The most important consequence of the reforms was the complete submission of the church to the state. In the nineteenth century, one can occasionally find demands for a restoration of the patriarchy and an episcopal guidance of the church. But they remained unfulfilled. The clergy fell into opposition to the hierarchy, and the intelligentsia put distance between it and the church — a relationship that was mutual. In the twentieth century, there were, indeed, isolated attempts to create contact between the church and the intelligentsia (like the famous "Religious-Philosophical Meetings in Petersburg" between 1901 and 1903); but they had no lasting effect. Most intellectuals and artists either had no religious interest at all, or the church played no large role in their understanding of religion. In this connection, one can list the so-called Searchers for God and the literary movement of symbolism. But the church was in no position to receive these currents. In 1917, at the end of its synodical phase, it was "in a miserable state."[2]

This situation also could not be changed by the possibilities engendered by the reforms of 1905. Now, for the first time, religious toleration was granted not only to foreigners and newly conquered people. More than 300,000 who had been forced to be Orthodox left the church as soon as it was possible. Pobedonostsev had to resign, but demands for a council did not prevail. A planning committee could be formed, but it was dissolved by the tsar after a brief time. There were tensions between the monks from whom the bishops were always selected in the Orthodoxy, and the secular clergy who had to do pastoral care. But they hardly

---

2. Konrad Onasch, *Grundzüge der russischen Kirchengeschichte* (Göttingen: Vandenhoeck & Ruprecht, 1967), M 12.

had any opportunity to advance. Various groupings arose among the laity who strove for a reform of the church, but none of the demands could be realized before World War II.

The Local Council of 1917

In August of 1917, the "local council" began in the Kremlin in Moscow, during the time of the "provisional government" after the abdication of the tsar and before the October Revolution. It not only reestablished the patriarchal office but also formulated numerous proposals for the organization of the church according to Orthodox principles. It stipulated the structures of how the Russian Church should enter the Soviet period. But it could not consolidate, indeed, could not even realize it, so that its influence remained negligible — aside from the reintroduction of the patriarchy.

The council could have recourse to what the planning committee had worked out ten years earlier. But it also inherited the problems and quarrels of the planning committee. Even the idea of reintroducing the office of the patriarch was controversial. Thus, shortly after the abdication of the tsar, some opposed the intention to introduce again a monarchical element into the church. The opponents were, above all, secular clergymen, professors of theological educational institutions, as well as some laypeople. There also were discussions about the establishment of a collective governing body that was to consist only of bishops. But finally, the supporters of a reintroduction prevailed, not only advancing historical reasons but also arguing for the necessity of rejecting the reforms of Peter.

The local council consisted of a majority of laymen (314 of 564 members). Two priests and three laymen from every diocese were delegates in addition to all the bishops and representatives of the monasteries, of the academies, and of the universities. The decisions of the plenary assembly were once more examined by the plenary assembly of the bishops and could be overturned by a three-quarter majority. This meant that the council had far-reaching rights and possibilities. The bishops could occupy, according to Orthodox ecclesiology, a central position in the church if they proceeded with great unanimity. The Kiev metropolitan, Antoniy (Khrapovitskiy), later the head of the church abroad, was the honorary chairman while the Moscow metropolitan, Tikhon (Belavin), was elected president.

The decision to reestablish the patriarchy was made on November 4, in the face of the revolutionary events in Petersburg and of the advance of the Bolsheviks on Moscow. The decision declared that the patriarch was to head the administration of the church, but that the local council, now institutionalized, possessed the highest authority in the church. The patriarch, "first among equals" *(primus inter pares)* among the bishops, was accountable to the council. After this decision, there was a vote about a list of three candidates for the office, for which lots were cast. Metropolitan Tikhon, who had received the least votes for the roster, drew the lot as the new patriarch. He was solemnly enthroned on November 21. After more than two hundred years, the Russian Church had, once again, a patriarch as its head. The synodical phase, frequently perceived as anomalous, had come to an end.

A core topic of the local council was the question of the participation of the laity in the government of the church, including democratic elements. The council tried to do justice to this concern with its decisions. Given the situation of the Russian Church, every decision had to involve innovations anyway. In the future, the bishops were to be appointed by a governing body in which priests and laymen were represented; parishes also obtained greater independence. Altogether, there is a clear emphasis on the synodical principle according to which decisions are made by governing bodies and in transparent procedures. The decisions of the council could never be realized because of the start of the revolution and the circumstances in the young Soviet Union. In September 1918, the new rulers forced it to end.

But afterward, the church never returned to the decisions of the council, and one must be indebted, above all, to Western research that they were not forgotten. The potential for reform, which, without doubt, can be found in the records and decisions of the council, has so far not been used. Today, it looks as if de facto more power should be given to the full assembly of the bishops and the synod, as it exists today, than to the local council, which is convened now only for the election of a new patriarch.

In the Soviet Union, the authorities tried, in connection with the efforts to destroy the Orthodox Church, to influence the ecclesiastical structure also through the state. The church, the diocese, or a priest was no longer regarded as being responsible for a parish, but a group of twenty believers (*dvadtsatka* in Russian) had to apply to the authorities for registration as a parish and for the use of a church building ("cult space"). The priest was (as "cult servant") an employee of this group with its right of initiative. In the background was the attempt to destroy the classical ecclesiology with the relation between priest and bishop and, in this way, also between parish and bishop. The church was no longer to exist as an organization but only as single individuals with the need to unite for the purpose of practicing religion. But this action was not successful. Even though it remained formally in force until the end of the Soviet Union, the authorities had to take the church into account as an organization, at least after World War II.

In the Soviet Union, the church was governed by a synod headed by a patriarch. A second patriarch, after Tikhon, could be elected in 1943, after an interval of eighteen years. The synod consisted of a patriarch and some bishops, some of whom belonged because of their office while others were added by election from time to time. It was evident that only bishops favored by the authorities could exercise this function, especially since there were hardly any other bishops in the entire country. The controlling authority was — besides the Secret Service — the Council for Religious Affairs.

At the end of the Soviet Union, the KGB (Committee of State Security) received a successor organization in the Russian Federation. It presumably is no longer occupied with the Orthodox Church, and the Council for Religious Affairs no longer exists. The ROC can now be an autonomous organization, not subject to external influences. But it has hardly changed its structures since the Soviet time. Above all, it has not realized the decisions of the local council of 1917.

The Russian Orthodox Church Today

The Russian Church today is comprised of more than 200 dioceses, among them a whole series in the "near abroad," that is, in the CIS and in the Baltic States, as well as in other countries abroad. The church founded dozens of dioceses within the last years, to provide better pastoral care for its believers, and it introduced a system of metropolitan sees covering the territory of Russia, so that we find now three levels: patriarchate, metropolitan see, diocese. In 2007, it had 136 dioceses; by 2012 it had around 230.

In the summer of 2000, the ROC defined its "canonical territory," which, accordingly, is comprised of all earlier republics of the USSR, with the exception of Armenia and Georgia, which have Orthodox churches of their own. In addition, according to this definition, all believers abroad belong to it if they volunteered to do so. In Belarus, where there is an "exarchate," and in Ukraine, the dioceses of the Russian Church administer themselves in a kind of autonomy but are not autonomous according to the sense of Orthodox canon law. The exarchates have their own respective synod headed by a metropolitan. His office makes him a member of the Moscow synod.

The highest organ of the church is the local council (*pomestnyy sobor* in Russian). It convenes de facto only for the election of a patriarch. It consists of all bishops and representatives of the clergy and the monks as well as the laity. The statutes of the church determine that all tasks of the local council can also be dealt with by the plenary assembly of the bishops, except the election of the patriarch. The most recent council convened in 2009 and elected the present patriarch, Kirill (Gundyayev). A local council was originally planned for the jubilee year 2000, but it did not convene. A plenary assembly of bishops took its place.

The plenary assembly of bishops, that is, the governing body of all bishops of the Russian Church, prepares the local council according to the regulations of the church. It carries out the decisions of the council; determines the regulations of the ROC; makes decisions about basic theological, canonical, liturgical, and pastoral questions; and makes decisions about canonizations and outside relations to which also belongs, for example, the establishment of exarchs. Plenary sessions are also relatively rare; since the election of Patriarch Alexiy, they have convened in 1992, 1994, 1997, 2000, 2004, 2008, and 2011. Another one has been announced for 2013. They arranged, above all, canonizations of saints, and created ecclesiastical institutions that were to confer new impulses to life in the church. The plenary assembly of 2000 canonized the last tsar and his family and, among other things, passed a much noticed document on social doctrine as well as a text on the relations to "heterodoxy," that is, to non-Orthodox Christianity.

Today, the church is de facto governed by the Holy Synod. This governing body consists of the patriarch, seven permanent bishops, and five alternating bishops. The permanent members are the metropolitans of Kiev, Minsk, St. Petersburg, Krutitskiy, and Kishinev (Chisinau); the head of the ecclesiastical external relations department; and the managing director of the patriarchy. The remaining members are appointed according to the principle of seniority for one session at a time, lasting half a year. The synod, therefore, is the executive organ of the church. It convenes regularly and makes decisions guided by the patriarch. The decisions are published in the *Journal of the Moscow Patriarchy;* they also can be found (in the original text and in English translation) on the Web site of the church.[3] A series of institutions are available to the synod, the most important of which are the Department for External Church Relations, the Theological Commission, the Council for Publications, a publishing house, the Teaching Committee, the Youth Committee, as well as the executive management of the patriarchy.

The patriarch, finally, leads the church according to the statute "together with the Holy Synod." He has an honorary precedence among the bishops. The local council elects him from the bishops of the ROC who are older than forty years. The patriarch enjoys high esteem among the believers, and in the protocol of the state he is listed today in second place after the president. But as far as ecclesiastical decisions are concerned, he is not more and not less, number one in the synod. He presides at the meetings, but has only one vote.

3. www.patriarchia.ru

CHAPTER FIVE

Church and State

S o far, we have shown that the relationship between the Orthodox
Church in Russia and the country's political systems has always been
of a special nature. The history of the church in Russia can hardly be
treated without parallel attention to the history of Russia; both are inti-
mately connected. Consequently, every Russian church history must always also keep an eye on the state. Certainly, the church is in a special position vis-à-vis the state because it can appeal to a much longer history. It
already existed before the Rus', and the Russian political systems cannot
readily be understood in the transpositions, reforms, and revolutions as
being identical with it.

The special character of the state-church relations concerns not only
the always recurring question of church property but also, and very basically, the way the church is tied to the political system (understood to be
Orthodox). Here, too, the Byzantine legacy produces an aftereffect that,
however, has received its own character through the events of modern
times. Still today, at a time when there are no preconditions on either
side, the church explicitly defines its relation to the state and the Russian
state tries to find a suitable relationship with Russian Orthodoxy. This
again moves observers at home and abroad to analyze this relation so that
continually discussions and evaluations occur. It is noteworthy that the
ROC identified itself in its history with the respective state, not so much
with the Russian nation, even though this is slowly changing in the present. This, too, has historical reasons.

Byzantine "Symphony" in the Rus' and in the Moscow Empire

The relation between church and state in the Byzantine Empire has been understood and described as "symphony" *(symphonia)*. This term says that both realities were regarded as different appearances of one and the same reality. They functioned in "harmony" for the same goal. A specialist in Byzantine studies, Hans G. Beck, has called this relationship very aptly "political Orthodoxy."[1] There are numerous examples of the actualization of this principle: the emperors convened councils, presided in them (at least in the important sessions), and had the decisions of them enacted in the empire; or the phenomenon that repeatedly occurred in Byzantine history where one of the high civil servants, who was a layman, was nominated to be patriarch and within a few days was consecrated to be deacon, priest, and bishop. But this certainly did not mean that the church in Byzantium (or in Russia) would have been simply subordinated to the state, or that the emperor would have had the highest sacral function in the sense of a caesaropapism (the state controlling the church). Both realms belonged to the Byzantine reality of life. A separation of the two was not at all conceivable, at least not by modern standards. This interweaving must be heeded if one wants to comprehend adequately the reality of Constantinople and also the one of Russian Church history. At the same time, a modern idea of the state can be applied only in a very restricted sense to the Byzantine Empire and hardly to the Kievan Rus'.

The beginnings of the Russian Church had a jurisdictional bond with Constantinople. It was expressed in the fact that in the liturgy not only the grand prince and the metropolitan were commemorated, but even before them the Byzantine emperor (after all, a foreign head of state!) and the patriarch of Constantinople. Only the growing self-consciousness of Moscow caused the abolition of this commemoration at the turn from the fourteenth to the fifteenth century.

The relation between the imperial court and the church in Kiev was shaped according to the Byzantine legacy. The prince determined de facto the conditions for the ecclesiastical framework. This would not be understood as a special limitation. The church was not in competition with the court but was rather a part of it. At diverse opportunities, the

---

1. The title of a chapter in his book *Das byzantinische Jahrtausend* (Munich: C. H. Beck, 1978).

princes negotiated with other rulers or representatives of Greek Orthodoxy about church affairs and frequently nominated the bishops. The Christianization itself also was not the result of successful missionary efforts but the consequence of public, political, and military actions. Conversely, the metropolitans could, at times, carry out political functions, above all, in difficult situations (like after the death of a prince); could be in charge of the regency; or, at least, could become engaged in stabilizing a situation and thus preserving continuity.

The policy of canonizations is another evidence for the relation between church and state. Until the Moscow period, the overwhelming part of all canonizations involved princes. The first of them were the brothers Boris and Gleb, who were canonized in the eleventh century. They were sons of Vladimir and lost their lives in battles for succession between his seven sons. Their brother Yaroslav the Wise, who became grand prince for the first time in 1019 and then ruled alone from 1036 until his death in 1054, saw to it that his brothers were canonized since it was believed that they had accepted death by their brother Svyatopolk with Christian humility and without resistance. This also involved a political decision: Yaroslav could claim legitimacy for his reign because the opponents of his rival were martyrs and the rival was their murderer, and for the stabilization of the dynasty that, in fact, he accomplished.

Canonizations always remained an instrument for political signals. At the synods in 1547 and 1549, many canonizations expressed the claim for Russian independence. Alexander Nevskiy, the victor against the Swedes and the Teutonic Order, became one of the most important saints of the Russian Church and was venerated as such after the fourteenth century. He was recalled again and again, above all, in times of pressure from the West, and he was portrayed not only as a Christian saint but also as a victorious prince and knight. The fact that he was a Christian saint did not even bother Stalin, who used him after the German attack of the USSR not only by means of the famous Eisenstein film but also on posters, pamphlets, and other media as a symbol of the victorious battle of Russia against the West.

The church gained a certain autonomy at the time of the Tartars. It enjoyed protection for its land and buildings as well as freedom from taxes. In addition, it was guaranteed freedom from persecution in accordance with Islamic religious law. To that extent, there was even a legal relationship between the Golden Horde and the Orthodox Church since these rights had been conceded in a formal document *(jarlig)*. The church was only required to pray for the Khan — an astonishing transaction because, after all, it involved the occupier of the land to whom the princes had to pay tribute. This creative continuation of the "symphony" corresponded quite well with the Orthodox idea of a state that protected the Orthodox Church and, therefore, could call for loyalty. Centuries later, the ecumenical patriarchs dealt hardly differently with the Ottoman rulers. So it is not surprising that later the church did not use the privileged position, enjoyed in the Tartar period, after the Russian independence, to ask the grand prince for similar autonomy. Such autonomy was no longer viewed as necessary under an Orthodox ruler.

In 1261, the church established a diocese in Sarai, the capital of the Golden Horde. This was done not for the purpose of mission but to further the influence of the church on the Golden Horde. This is a further sign of the autonomy granted the church by the Mongols. At this time, the church, not the princes, was the uniting bond for the Rus'. But this did not mean at all a victory of the church in a weak phase of the state. It rather meant that, at a time of distress, the church, as one of two elements complementing one another, and being of central significance for the Rus', recognized its responsibility for the common welfare. No dispute between the two can be inferred regarding a leading role.

The increasing importance of Moscow and the growing power of the political system also created ideas that contributed to a theological basis for the stature of Moscow. Reference has already been made to the perception of Moscow as the third Rome. Here, the symbolical suggestions of a transfer of the significance of Byzantium after its fall must also be noted, among them the marriage of Grand Prince Ivan III to a niece of the last Byzantine emperor. The sources are now using more and more the notion of *tsarstvo*, tsardom, empire, representing a translation of the Greek *basileia;* thus, it has a religious connotation since it refers to the New Testament notion of the kingdom of God. Every Orthodox liturgy begins with a praise of the *tsarstvo* of the Father, the Son, and the Holy Spirit. That is why the mention of one's own state as *tsarstvo* could not simply be understood in a neutral sense.

How did the church behave in this new situation? It had gained canonical independence from Constantinople after the Council of Florence and its consequences. So there now was an independent church in an increasingly powerful state. There was a discussion about the stance of the church among the monks, and it must be viewed in connection with the dispute about church property between Nil and Joseph. The church had to make a final decision between supporting the state and withdrawing into asceticism. Even though the ascetic orientation has a basis in the Orthodox tradition, it is nevertheless to be anticipated, in view of the church-state tradition, in which direction the decision could only go. The ecclesiastical literature of the time contains admonitions to the grand princes to respect the rights of the church as well, as also (and included in them) eschatologically colored notions that understand the Moscow empire as the last empire. Consequently, there is a warning about infringements of the established tradition — a stance that was actualized again and again in the form of resistance against innovations, above all, against those from Western foreign countries. This was, to be sure, not a public policy but, nevertheless, a motif found frequently in the church.

This example shows well that the notion of the historical space comprises not only the existing "structural space" and politically altered "mapped space," but also the "perceived space." The realm, formed by geographical realities, above all, structured by the courses of rivers and shaped by "the gathering of the Russian land," is perceived as a divinely willed unity, as an eschatological empire. It goes without saying that this also legitimizes political rule.

Under Ivan IV ("the Terrible"), the Russian state not only attained a new form but also strengthened its orientation to the church based on the Byzantine model. It was expressed (only after Ivan's death) in the elevation to the patriarchy in 1589. On the whole, the Greek model now became weaker and weaker. On the one hand, the Byzantine Empire had become history, after more than a century, and Greeks could not be an ideal because they lived under the Ottomans. On the other hand, after the victory of the Josephites, the orientation on the Byzantine model had become problematical because the monasteries were not as significant for the state there.

The metropolitan of Moscow, Makariy (1482-1563), contributed, above all, to the strengthened emphasis of the Moscow idea of the state. He emphasized the Russian ecclesiastical tradition, and under his auspices the above-mentioned canonizations were accomplished. He made brief readings available, "Menaions" (Greek for "monthly readings"), which were arranged according to the calendar so that they could be read continuously in the liturgy and in the monasteries. They had strong Russian features and supported a providential view of the Russian political system: it was divine providence that made the Moscow empire what it was. In 1547, Makariy assisted in the coronation of Ivan IV as tsar; it was done according to the Byzantine ritual, after the approval of the title by the patriarch of Constantinople. The metropolitan exercised great influence over the (sixteen-year-old) tsar, who exhibited the cruelty linked to his name only after the death of the metropolitan.

Ivan IV understood his own role as divinely willed. Qualified by his theological education, he conducted theological disputes with the Catholic envoy Antonio Possevino, a Jesuit, who stayed in Moscow for a few months in 1582. The church had its firm place in the political system; it was the guardian of the handed-down legacy and, at the same time, supporter of the tsar. In this sense, it differed from the Greek tradition. This did not become evident to Possevino, who considered the Russian Church to be a variation of the "Greek faith."

The question of the relation to the Greek model became ever more pressing in time. The various versions of the liturgical books contributed, above all, to it because they originated through mistakes in copying and through differing translations. The differences became evident in the contacts with the Greek realm and with the Orthodox Christians on the Balkan Peninsula. In Moscow, the synods of 1525 and 1531 dealt with this question, which was to become even more virulent through the first editions (after 1563) because they now could be standardized. The question of the production of the editions was finally to cause a dispute and the break with the Old Believers.

The dilemma between the older Greek and the Russian traditions also applied to the Hundred-Chapter Synod of 1551, which originated through an initiative not of the church but of the state: the tsar had made concrete inquiries to which the bishops formulated answers. They showed the restraining and conservative attitude of the Russian Church, and they moved, in part, far away from the tradition of the Greek Church. The stipulation of Russian customs, for example, the "two-finger cross," in which the sign of the cross is made with two fingers, served as a strong argument of the Old Believers more than a century later when the church turned more to the Greek models and, accordingly, prescribed the "three-finger cross."

Thus, early Russian church history shows an almost symbiotic relation between state and church. This is, to be sure, not a Russian invention but continues the tradition of the "symphony." In the course of Russian history, specific elements were added that marked the church-state relation in Russia until the end of the seventeenth century. The variation is also the consequence of the rise of modern nations that were no longer just strongly guided by the person who ruled. The origin of an administration, an institutionalization, and similar phenomena are the results. In Russia, this development is strongly connected with Peter I and his reforms.

The Russian Church and the Enlightened State

Ideas of the European Enlightenment entered Russia with the reforms of Peter. His changes of the ecclesiastical structure, which were the most incisive in Russian church history, initiated a turning point. Administrative force broke the enduring resistance of the church against all Western influences. The church was forced to enter a system it perceived as strange and inappropriate; but it had no means to resist. To that extent, it is not surprising that people today in Russian Orthodoxy see in these changes, indeed in the European Enlightenment, a basic malady, and would love to transfer the church into an epoch before Peter. This attitude often overlooks the fact that historical developments cannot be rendered null and void.

The first successors of Peter were weak, for the most part, and did not govern a long time. When Catherine II ("the Great") came into power, she developed his ideas further and tried, also in regard to the church, to have her enlightened attitude accepted. Her husband and immediate predecessor was Tsar Peter III, a converted Lutheran of German-Russian descent, who governed only for half a year. He tried, without success, to make the church Protestant, by prohibiting, for example, icons and by ordering priests to shave and wear civilian clothes. What he did accomplish in 1762 was the secularization of the ecclesiastical possessions that his predecessors had been trying to attain in vain for many centuries. The church, of course, tried to resist but was no longer in a position to do so. Almost a million peasants and their families, who had hitherto "belonged" to the church, now became free as "state peasants"; the land they had cultivated became the property of a state authority. More than 600 of over 1,000 monasteries were closed. Two years later, these measures were completely enforced by his widow.

Catherine II, born as German princess Sophie of Anhalt-Zerbst, was influenced by French rationalism and the Enlightenment. In contrast to Peter, she had no religious interests. She had, of course, converted to Orthodoxy, but she did not come from an Orthodox tradition and deemed Orthodoxy and Protestantism to be religious trends in very close proximity to each other. She viewed the church as a secular institution that had to be subject to the state and its interests. This was a modification in comparison to the "common good" that had still been in the forefront for Peter. On the basis of his point of view, she could also designate herself the "head of the church."

On the one hand, the measures of Catherine II had negative financial consequences for the church. On the other hand, they were also connected with the claim to elevate the level of education. The tsarina completed the secularization of the ecclesiastical possessions begun by her predecessor and broke the resistance that came, above all, from the bishops who frequently were originally from Ukraine. Consequently, more sees were now again occupied by Russians. There was still scattered resistance from the clergy, but hardly from the episcopate. The rationale for the measures of dispossession was the state's understanding of the church as a public institution whose proceeds belong to the state (aside from one-sixth left to the church). Increased expenses of the state, especially for warlike enterprises, were the factual reason. Now the church, also with regard to finances, was no longer on a par with the state.

The enlightened posture was connected not only with Orthodoxy but basically also with every kind of religion. An Edict of Toleration, issued in 1773, granted relative freedom to other religions and Christian denominations. The spread of the Old Believers could no longer be prevented. Their successful merchants were important for the state so that the measures, imposed on them, were relaxed. Jesuits, who had been prohibited by Rome, were invited to Russia and could get organized. Dioceses were established for Catholics. But their purpose was, in the first place, to receive the Uniates, whose church was suppressed. Russia had expanded its borders to the west and, in the process, received, besides many Jews, people of the Greek Catholic Church; that, however, was not tolerated. In the "Great Instruction" of 1766, Catherine listed the "tranquility and peace of the subjects" as reasons for the necessity of religious toleration in a large empire with many peoples under its rule.

In 1786, the ecclesiastical and public school systems were separated from each other. Consequently, the financing of the parochial schools was improved. The original idea of placing theology at the university (the first one had been founded in 1755 in Moscow) was no longer pursued. Instead, value was set on improving the education of priests. The number of diocesan schools grew. Attendance was forced by allowing the sons of priests to attain the office of their fathers only if they graduated from such a school. And if they did not, they had to do military service. At the turn from the eighteenth to the nineteenth century, there were forty-two such schools. It is significant that most of them were in Ukraine. The schools were afflicted by numerous problems: frequently, the clergy did not understand the need of education; the instruction was often in Latin, which the students could hardly understand; and strict discipline ruled. Yet, on the whole, the schools helped raise the level of education, especially since they often represented the only opportunity to receive an education. Ultimately, educated priests were a goal of the enlightened state.

The priests earned their living from payments for administering sacraments and other official acts, from the salary they obtained from their parish, as well as — and often above all — from the land made available to them, which they cultivated as other parish members did, often neglecting their pastoral tasks. In the nineteenth century, attempts were made to let priests have a public salary, but without enduring success; frequently, the clergy continued to live in extremely modest circumstances. De facto, parishes could be inherited, a practice in Russia (but not in Ukrainian territories), supported by the hierarchy until the second half of the nineteenth century. It led to the creation of something like a "caste of priests," a social class that frequently had little connection with the rest of society and whose social mobility was extremely limited. The isolated education of the priests also was a contributing cause. That is why, as a rule, their social reputation was not very high. After a reform of seminaries in 1867, sons of priests had an opportunity to choose other professions. As a result, educated priests became scarce and candidates with an inadequate education were frequently ordained, a situation that was to mark the church until the revolution of 1917. On the other hand, learned monks were frequently nominated bishops in the synodical phase. But they had neither pastoral nor monastic experience.

The subordination of the church to the state became visible in numerous, often symbolical, details. The tsars were crowned by the metropolitan of the capital and anointed according to the Byzantine tradition (at times, the Eastern church viewed this act even as a sacrament). But the emperor himself placed the crown on his head: he was the autocrat who did not receive his authority from anyone but ruled strictly on his own. Priests could be forced to surrender the secrecy of the private confession when it was a question of crimes against the state. The well-being of the state was first and foremost.

Under these circumstances, the Russian Church became an established church in the sense that it was subordinated to the state and dependent on it. It was a totally different situation than the one of state and church being together, as was the rule since the beginning. An important reason was the church's insistence on rejecting all changes, especially those that came from the West. The basically necessary development and the adjustment to changing circumstances were introduced through public measures against the will of the church. The church could no longer influence the state that financed it to a considerable degree in the nineteenth century; it also could not have any influence on its internal structure.

The self-understanding of the Russian state was characterized in the now famous formula "Autocracy, Orthodoxy, Nationality" *(samoderzhaviye, pravoslaviye, narodnost')* of Sergey Uvarov, the Minister for the Public Education under Nikolay I (1833-49). The monarchic form of government was understood as neither granted nor derived. In addition, Orthodoxy was one of the elements that constituted and marked the state, and also the Russian national character (it is difficult to translate the term *narodnost'*). The religious dimension seems to play hardly a role anymore because the church was understood as an institution that upheld and maintained the state.

The Governing Synod became more and more the means used by the state to control the church. Peter I and Feofan Prokopovich, the creator of the Synod, did not plan it that way. They wanted to create an ecclesiastical instrument to lead the church and to maintain it within the new political system, but the possibility of controlling the church through the state was already arranged in the function of the chief procurator and realized in the nineteenth century. The office of the Chief Secretary of the Consistory was also instituted; these officers were the representatives of the Synod in the individual dioceses that the bishops could control.

The Church under Communism

The revolution of 1917 radically changed a basic presupposition that had not been disputed up to that time; the new Communist state viewed the church as an enemy it wanted to annihilate. For numerous devout citizens, it could do so all at once, and it did not take the state long to almost completely destroy the church. So the church was, for the first time, in a situation where the rulers not only did not belong to it, but would not even tolerate it. In the view of the revolutionaries, the church was not only not important but also obstructive for the well-being and prosperity of the state.

It is understandable that the separation of state and church, as well as church and school, was one of the first measures after the revolution. The original idea of simply declaring religion a private affair was changed by Lenin's personal intervention with his own hand in the laconic first sentence of the Decree, "The church is separated from the state." But although, de facto, the church separated from the state, the state was not separated from the church. It interfered again and again in the affairs of the church, directly or indirectly, whenever it seemed right. The church, on the other hand, had no possibility to affect the state in any way.

Already in the summer of 1917, under the provisional government, the state increasingly withdrew from ecclesiastical affairs. The office of the chief procurator was dissolved and replaced by a government department for confessions of faith that considered the Orthodox Church an autonomous corporation. Freedom of religion was legally defined, thus ending the privileged position of Orthodoxy. Parochial schools were extracted from the ecclesiastical supervision and put under the authority of a government department. But all these arrangements remained in force for only a few months.

After October 1917, the Communist government nationalized all land still belonging to the church and transferred all schools to the People's Commissar for Public Education. Births and weddings now were also a matter of public record. Religious instruction was prohibited. Any reference to religion within the realm of the state was forbidden, for example, in court, and religious communities became private associations, without any right to have property. Church buildings, therefore, became the property of the state, made available when needed, as defined by the state.

A brief time of cautious waiting on both sides was quickly followed by a far-reaching persecution of the organized Orthodox Church. The Bolsheviks, however, supported other churches when it was opportune for them. So they established cautious relations with the Vatican during the great famine of 1921-22. A papal relief mission was sent to Russia. In Ukraine, the Bolsheviks supported a noncanonical Ukrainian Orthodox Church that regarded itself as an expression of national emancipation from Russian domination.

The smoldering conflict between state and church escalated in the quest for the release of liturgical objects that were to be sold in order to purchase food for easing the famine. The state used the refusal of the church to make consecrated objects available as an occasion to act massively against it. Public propaganda against religion became increasingly louder, and more and more priests were sentenced to death. Finally, Patriarch Tikhon (Belavin) was arrested in May of 1922 and held in custody for over a year. While he was detained, a "Declaration of Loyalty," supposedly written by him, was published in the newspapers; it is considered a forgery today. In it he supposedly declared himself "no longer an enemy to the Soviet power." But after his release, an orderly government of the church was no longer possible. After his death in 1925, a testament was published, probably also forged, in which he appealed to the believers of his church to be loyal to the Soviet Union.

The state proceeded against the church on two levels. First, priests and members of monasteries were arrested, condemned, and killed in great numbers. In the first five years of Soviet rule, the church lost about 23,000 priests, monks, and nuns, among them a few dozen bishops. Many others were confined to camps that had been equipped for clergymen on the Solovki Islands in the White Sea. In addition, numerous churches and monasteries were closed. Church government was unable to function properly because most of the members of synods were imprisoned, and after Tikhon's death, none of the three deputies he had appointed could do this task until a new patriarch was elected. In addition, measures appeared, targeting the believers, such as the abolition of the public protection of church holidays, or the attempt (later retracted) to make Sunday an ordinary working day.

Second, the state supported groups who split the church. The Renewers, also known as "Living Church," were people who came from the church, among them two priests who sympathized with the Bolsheviks and demanded ecclesiastical reforms. They went far beyond much that was seriously debated at the local council of 1917: modern Russian should be used as liturgical language rather than Old Slavonic; priests should also marry after their ordination, that is, be able to marry again after having been widowed; bishops should be allowed to marry; and the liturgy should be shortened. The Renewers were massively supported by the state. Their relatives were exempted from persecution, indeed appeared as witnesses for the prosecution against priests. After the arrest of Tikhon, they were enabled to take over the administration of the patriarchy. Church buildings were especially at their disposal. They declared Tikhon deposed, and they themselves revoked excommunications imposed on them.

The Renewers received hardly any encouragement from believers, even though some bishops and priests joined them and established a synod that was replaced by a patriarch in 1935. Known scandals about leading members of the movement and general restraint about proposals for innovation, above all, when they were radical, may have contributed to this. After 1925, public support diminished, when it became clear that the Renewers would not be able to bring the whole church under their control. When the general terror increased in the 1930s, it did not exempt the Renewers. Some remained priests and bishops in the Church of the Renewers until the 1940s, at which time it disappeared from history.

It is not easy to grasp the motivations of the Renewers. Personal dissatisfactions, as well as the attempt to link religiosity with socialist views, certainly played an important role. The Renewers reached back for formulations of questions that, in their view, had not been satisfactorily resolved by the local council of 1917. They thought Orthodoxy was no longer viable in its existing form and had to change radically to have a place in society under the new political circumstances. The authorities, on the other hand, never were interested in a church, no matter how it would be suited to Bolshevism. Their first goal was the destruction of the unity of the Russian Church, especially since they knew that an estrangement of all believers from the church could not be achieved in a short time.

Neither the cautious attempts of Patriarch Tikhon for a rapprochement with the regime nor the famous declaration of loyalty by Metropolitan Sergiy (Stragorodskiy) in 1927 preserved the church from further persecution. A law of religion in 1929 limited all religious activities to the "cult," that is, to worship within church buildings; this prohibited any other form of pastoral care. Likewise, religious instruction for persons younger than eighteen was prohibited, as well as for groups. Only single catechesis was possible for adults. The collectivization of agriculture brought religious life in the village almost completely to a standstill. Totally contrary to these events, the Constitution of the USSR guaranteed in 1936 all citizens "freedom for the exercise of religious cult activities and freedom for anti-religious propaganda."[2]

2. The text of the Constitution was published in 1937 in Moscow in English

When the rulers realized that religion would not disappear by itself nor through the measures used up to that time, they increased the propaganda. "Atheism" was declared a scientific discipline for which professorial chairs were established where methods of natural science were to prove that there is no God and that religion is a product of the human imagination. Groups and movements were created, such as the "Godless" and the "Militant Atheists," and numerous publications dealt with the topic. At the same time, the cult of heroes was intensified to assist in picking up religious elements. Since the terror of the 1930s, it has become difficult to distinguish between a religious and a general persecution.

The attitude of the Soviet state toward the Orthodox Church changed for pragmatic reasons. On June 22, 1941, German armed forces assaulted the USSR. On the same day (more than a week before Stalin did so!), Metropolitan Sergiy summoned all shepherds and believers in a circular letter to fight the intruders.[3] The church organized collections among the believers and contributed substantial sums to the Defense Fund for financing weapons for the Red Army. Special donations financed a column of tanks, named "Dmitriy Donskoy," after the victor against the Tartars, and a squadron of planes, called "Alexander Nevskiy," after the conqueror of the Swedes and of the Teutonic Order.

Metropolitan Sergiy's action reflects significantly on the relation between state and church in the Russian tradition. The Soviet state had almost completely persecuted and destroyed the church. But in the face of an external threat, the church immediately and without reservation stood at its side. Only in the territories occupied by the Germans were there representatives of the church who cooperated with the occupiers. This was not least connected with the ecclesiastical politics of the German authorities, who intentionally promoted the churches in order to gain the confidence of the population and to guide the sentiment against Soviet rule. But on the whole, the church supported the fight of the USSR. This did not indicate an approval of the crimes committed by the regime but was, at best, a sign of recognizing the reality of Soviet rule. Above all,

---

("Constitution [Fundamental Law] of the Union of Soviet Socialist Republics": Partizdat). It is available at http://www.marxists.org/reference/archive/stalin/works/1936/12/05.htm (accessed August 8, 2012).

3. Text in Peter Hauptmann and Gerd Stricker, eds., *Die Orthodoxe Kirche in Russland. Dokumente ihrer Geschichte (860-1980)* (Göttingen: Vandenhoeck & Ruprecht, 1988), 750-51.

it showed that the state was recognized as "Russian" and, therefore, was for the church the state it acknowledged as its own.

The state accepted the support of the church. The active attempts to make the existence of the church impossible stopped. In 1943, there was a historic meeting between three bishops and Stalin at which the church was permitted to elect a new patriarch. After eighteen years as the deputy of the office, Metropolitan Sergiy was appointed as the successor of Tikhon, but he died after a few months. His successor could also be elected, Alexiy I (Simanskiy), who headed the church until 1970. After his death, Patriarch Pimen (Izvekov) was elected in 1971. His successor was Patriarch Alexiy II (Ridiger), who governed the church from 1990 until 2008. The present Patriarch Kirill (Gundyayev) followed him in 2009.

The authorities also allowed the church to engage in previously prohibited activities. It could publish the *Journal of the Moscow Patriarchy* and some books, and establish again institutions for the education of priests. Ecclesiastical life was slowly consolidated, albeit on a low standard. Frequently, trustworthy men were ordained without an education for the priesthood because of the scarcity of priests; they continued their studies later through correspondence courses and earned the necessary degree. As a consequence of World War II, the USSR gained additional territories in the West that previously had belonged to Poland and had been occupied by the Germans. There, the flowering ecclesiastical life remained untouched so that the number of parishes and, above all, the number of monasteries of the ROC increased by leaps and bounds. In addition, the Greek Catholic Church in the western Ukraine was dissolved by force in 1946 and forced to join Russian Orthodoxy. This, too, powerfully increased the number of parishes. In the succeeding decades, most parishes of Russian Orthodoxy were to be located in the western Ukraine, and the largest number of priests came from there.

The religious policy of the Soviet government basically changed after the war. The church no longer needed to endure any direct measures of persecution. To begin with, the state accepted the church as a reality that existed in the USSR, and it tried to bring it under control through administrative measures. The church had greater opportunities to act, or better put, it had general opportunities to act, compared with the time immediately before the war. A Council for the Affairs of the Orthodox Church at the Cabinet Council of the USSR emerged. It was soon renamed Council on Religious Affairs. There were analogous councils in the Soviet Republics and the "districts" *(oblast')*. This regulated the relations between both sides, even though not on the same eye level. If the church felt that it was treated unjustly or arbitrarily, it could address the issue with the authorities. Besides, the arbitrariness that had ruled before the war no longer existed in this form. Antiecclesiastical measures at least appeared in the guise of "legality."

In connection with de-Stalinization, begun under Nikita Khrushchev in the 1950s, a sharper course was plotted again toward the church. It represented a balance with the "hawks," as it were. Stalin enjoyed a high esteem among many people, despite the terror. He was viewed, on the one hand, as the victor of World War II and, on the other hand, as someone who enforced order. That is why a return to the cult of personality and other elements of Stalinist politics was prudently accompanied by an antiecclesiastical course. Thus, numerous parishes and monasteries were closed in the late 1950s and early 1960s, among them the Kiev Cave Monastery, and bishops who were "too active" were sent into retirement. The state also tried to infiltrate the church. Agents of the Secret Service were channeled into seminaries, and attempts were made to persuade active priests and bishops to cooperate with the Secret Service. There was no access to the archives of the Secret Service in Russia after the end of Communism. But single documents revealed that some bishops not only shared information in conversations with collaborators of the KGB but also were members of the Service. But this had been surmised anyway in the West about most of those in question.

The Soviet Union also tried to use the ROC for its foreign policy objectives. Ecumenical relations were one of the instruments. Already in 1948, there was an assembly of Orthodox representatives in Moscow where the ecumenical movement was vehemently rejected, as was any contact with the Catholic Church. Then, in 1961, Russian Orthodoxy joined the World Council of Churches, and representatives were sent to Rome for the Second Vatican Council (1962-65). Today, these relations are intensely debated. Without doubt, the representatives of the Russian Church had to communicate the viewpoint of the government at international meetings. But also, without doubt these meetings presented an opportunity (perhaps the only one) to maintain contact with representatives of foreign churches, and this opportunity was also used beyond the formal and official level. In this context, the Leningrad metropolitan, Nikodim (Rotov), was an important personality. He had led the ROC into the World Council of Churches in 1961 and had intensified the ecumenical relations with the Catholic Church. It is also true that during the time of Leonid Brezhnev, who followed Khrushchev as chief of state and of the party, cautious openings in the society were accompanied by restrictions of activity in the realm of the church. The patriarch and the bishops had to justify Soviet politics and to deny restrictions of religious freedom, but the party had to notice again and again that there was an interest in religious questions especially on the part of younger people. In 1975, a report from the Council on Religious Affairs reached the West. It described the situation of the church as seen by the authorities. The report divided the bishops into three groups: those who were loyal and patriotic; those who were loyal but active in the church; and those who sought "to bypass the cult laws." Even after so many decades of different attitudes toward the church, the state did not succeed in bringing it under total control. But the church officially supported the peace campaign of the USSR not only verbally but also conceptually through conferences at which religious representatives affirmed disarmament, and materially through financial contributions to public funds for peace. Patriarch Pimen (1971-90), bearer of the Order of the Red Banner of Labor, enjoyed the same privileges as the members of the Politburo, and in case of sickness he was treated in the hospital for celebrities in the Kremlin. Although the church hardly improved its situation at home by this good conduct, it could maintain international contacts.

In the Soviet Union, the frame of ecclesiastical activity was always stipulated by the state. As long as the church accepted that, it could act; if it tried to go beyond that, it was stopped. There were hierarchs who adhered to these boundaries very strictly. But others tried to make the most of this elbow room and even tried to extend it. The government authorities, for their part, tried to bring the church under state control, above all, through administrative measures. Laypeople who were religiously engaged often had to endure disadvantages. This applied, above all, to younger people and to members of "sensitive" vocations, such as teachers, and to the intelligentsia. If priests and bishops attracted the negative attention of the authorities through intensive activities, or unpopular remarks, there was pressure for ecclesiastical punishment in most cases. Today, the church is at times blamed for compromising itself because of having been too close to the state in the Soviet period. But, on the one hand, the relation to the state is to be seen in the background of Russian tradition and history. On the other hand, an evaluation of the attitude of the church, especially from an outside perspective, seems to be extremely difficult, given the extraordinary circumstances to which it was exposed. Regarding the attitude of the church during and after the period of persecution from 1959 to 1964, the saying of Metropolitan Nikodim was handed on that the state must never again notice that it can manage to exist without the church. Being close and loyal to the state meant a certain restraint of the state through the church; now the state could no longer conduct itself as it did before World War II.

Church and National Identity after 1991

The millennial celebration of the baptism of the Rus' in 1988 marked a turning point for the ROC. Whereas Soviet politics of *perestroika* was still restrained toward the church, as, after all, also was the attitude of the church toward Gorbachev, now both sides showed a readiness to move toward each other. Representatives of the church were members in the Supreme Soviet, which was assigned great power by the head of the party. After the death of Patriarch Pimen, who was considered a representative of the bygone epoch, the relatively young and internationally experienced Metropolitan Alexiy was elected as the new patriarch. In 1990, the Soviet Union passed a very liberal law of religion, granting all religious communities great liberties so that also the prohibited Greek Catholic Church in Ukraine could exist again. Many people immediately declared their allegiance to it. Previously they had been members of Russian Orthodoxy, which now suffered serious losses of members and entire parishes.

The church experienced a public revaluation like never before. Ecclesiastical themes appeared in the media. Representatives of the church could speak their mind in front of microphones and cameras, and Russians became informed about forgotten religious customs and doctrines. Many people agreed to be baptized, new parishes were established, and public lectures about religious topics enjoyed great popularity. The changes of the twentieth century can be clearly shown in statistics of the number of Orthodox parishes on the territory of the Russian Empire, of the USSR, and of the CIS.[4]

4. For 1914: Hans-Christian Diedrich and others, eds., *Das Gute behaltet. Kirchen und religiöse Gemeinschaften in der Sowjetunion und ihren Nachfolgestaaten* (Erlangen: Martin Luther-Bund, 1996), 30; for 1940: Gerd Stricker, *Religion in Russland. Darstellung und Daten zu Geschichte und Gegenwart* (Gütersloh: Gütersloher Verlagshaus, 1993), 91; for 1946-91: Nathaniel Davis, *A Long Walk to Church: A Contemporary History of Russian Orthodoxy* (Boulder, Colo.: Westview Press, 1995), 112; for 2010: http://www.patriarchia.ru/db/text/1402889.html (accessed August 6, 2012).

Year	Parishes	Changes	Explanation
1914	40,000		
1940	below 500		
1946	10,504		Many of them originated in territories occupied by the German armed forces
1947	14,039	+34%	Forced integration of the Greek Catholic Church
1958	13,415	-5%	"Thaw" period
1966	7,466	-44%	Persecution under Khrushchev
1986	6,742	-10%	"Stagnation." Relaxation of the persecution
1991	10,118	+50%	After the *perestroika,* end of USSR
1999	19,065	+88%	
2001	22,800	+20%	Territory of the former USSR (including the Baltic States)
2007	27,393	+20%	
2010	30,675	+10%	

After freedom of religion was granted, religious communities, whose activities had been limited or totally prohibited, could exist as they had been, or as totally new ones. Arriving from Asia and North America, many sects began their activity in Russia, often using large sums of money. The Roman Catholic Church became active where it had been prohibited, even in regions where there had never been Catholics. All this, as well as the revival of the Union in Ukraine, was perceived as a threat by the ROC. For there were indeed a series of people who had been Orthodox before, or not at all religious, who had now become members of these religious communities. Russian Orthodoxy was unable to oppose these developments, neither with finances, nor with personnel, nor with concepts.

In the summer of 1991, an attempted coup against the head of state, Mikhail Gorbachev, resulted in the dissolution of the USSR at the end of the year. Some bishops of the Russian Church had supported the coup, others had rejected it. When in 1993 another coup was attempted against Russian President Yeltsin, something similar could be observed. This shows that the church was divided in itself. It had not only representatives who welcomed the democratization of the country, but also those who desired a return to the old, and presumably stable, circumstances. It demonstrated that Russian Orthodoxy was in a difficult situation when obscure public situations forced it to define its position.

Soon, the Russian Federation took charge of part of the functions for the church that had been traditionally in the hands of the state. This was first disclosed in 1997, when a new law of religion was passed. It was considerably more restrictive than the one before, although it granted significant simplifications, as the law put it, to "traditional" religions, namely, to Orthodoxy, Islam, Judaism, and Buddhism. Practice demonstrated that other Christian churches could find the opportunity to exist legally in Russia, although concrete interpretation of the laws is always dependent on the local authorities. But practice also showed that the state is given an instrument with which to proceed, more or less severely, against disagreeable religious communities.

There is evidence for a continuation of a kind of "symphony" tradition also in the reality of a religious pluralism in Russia. This is true for the government of the Russian presidents to date, Yeltsin, Putin, and Medvedev. The Orthodox Church as a majority church is, de facto, treated as an institution strongly connected with the state. It receives tax privileges in order to be able to finance itself. There are chapels and spiritual care in state institutions like the army, the police, and the Secret Service. The patriarch is present in a prominent position when the president is sworn in. Before a decision was made about religious instruction in the schools, the political authorities introduced in many locations a subject titled "Foundations of Orthodox Culture." It is a compulsory subject for all students, irrespective of their religious affiliation. Teachers of this subject are educated by newly established professorial chairs for "culturology." Both the state and the church try to convey an impression of Russia as a traditionally and primarily Orthodox country. Russia, to be sure, is indeed traditionally and primarily an Orthodox country. But it also has the (though forced) tradition of atheism, which today allows many people to be religiously indifferent, and there are members of religious minorities. For this very reason, these measures appear as an inappropriate preference for Orthodoxy by the state.

In the summer of 2000, the assembly of bishops of the ROC published an extensive document titled "Foundations of the Social Doctrine of the Russian Orthodox Church."[5] It deals with many topics from almost

---

5. The text is available in English at http://www.mospat.ru/en/documents/social -concepts/ (accessed August 8, 2012).

all areas of individual and social ethics, including the relation of the church to the state. In this document, the church describes the state as necessary in a fallen world and demands from believers — with reference to Romans 13 — obedience to the state and prayer for it, independent of the convictions of belief of the bearers of political power. It condemns the absolute state and demands from it protection of religion. The "symphony" is described as the model, but the church would have to fulfill the will of Christ in every form of the state and be loyal to the state; this would be true even for the state that persecutes the church. But also the ideologically neutral state would have to grant the church its realm of activity. The document even concedes a right of insubordination in case the state wants to force individual Christians, or the church, to act against conscience. On the whole, the text interprets the development from the theocratic circumstances in ancient Israel to the present democracies as symptoms of decay.

It is evident that the ROC had to search for a new role in society after the end of Communism, and obviously has not yet found it. The relations between church and state, to be sure, always have two sides, so that they cannot be defined by the church alone. The attitude of the state must also be considered. The Russian Federation is also interested in defining itself since the previously considered public values had mostly become invalid with the end of Communism. The previous president Yeltsin even had an open competition organized, searching countrywide for a national idea for Russia. The church, as representative of traditional values, and as an institution that already existed in prerevolutionary Russia, offers itself as a partner in order to confer a uniting sense to the state. In this context, it is problematic that there was a long interruption in the Russian ecclesiastical tradition and that the church is not equipped for the challenges of modernity without further ado.

There is, then, a specific relation between church and state in Russia. It evolved from the historical legacy of Byzantium, which had developed further under special Russian circumstances, and shows its dominance despite all the various events in Russian history. This relation distinguishes itself, in some respects, basically from the models that had originated in the Christian West. But there is a phenomenon at stake, shared by all Christian traditions: states look for a historical legitimization. This is even more important for modern rulers and their systems of governing than for premodern ones and their systems of dominance. Even though the West did not know a "symphony," Western examples can be found, above all, in modern times. They are not much different from this Byzantine model. This is true for states with a Catholic tradition, such as Spain and — with limitations — Austria, even until well into the twentieth century. This is also true for the model of the established church, for example, in Scandinavia or in the German principalities. In the West, a lengthy and difficult process ended this close mutual relation. It no longer exists today, with the process of separation initiated mostly by states and not by churches. At the same time, the significance of religion has declined in most western European societies. In Russia, there was a violent and, on the part of the church, involuntary separation of church and state, after long centuries of great proximity to the state. Today, the church is again consulted in the search for a new identity of the state. It can be surmised that, in this regard, the ROC will have to repeat the painful way of the Western churches. It will have to find its role in a democratic and plural society into which Russia — despite all detours — develops. But it is important that all attempts to explain the role of the ROC in state and society must pay heed to the complexity of the Russian church-state relation in history.

CHAPTER SIX

Theology and Religious Thought

The theology of Russian Orthodoxy must be understood in the greater context of Orthodox theology in general. This concerns, above all, the "prolegomena," the theological doctrine of principles. There are some basic statements about theology that imprint Orthodox theology and have been common to it since the time of the church fathers. Russian theology obviously took over these basic statements from Byzantium and has preserved them for a long time. But already in the early epoch, specific aspects differentiate the tradition from the Byzantine one.

The Byzantine Legacy

Orthodox theology views the church fathers and their theology as normative; the tradition of the church is concentrated and manifested in them. On the other hand, the church fathers claimed not to develop a new theology but to offer an authentic interpretation of the message of Christ, handed down in Holy Scripture and the apostolic tradition. A far-reaching hermeneutical problem exists behind these two basic statements: it can only be indicated here. The theology of the Fathers did not arrive in the present unchanged. It is not possible to preserve the identity of theological viewpoints across many centuries and in completely different situations and contexts. Even if the wording is unchanged, they still necessarily undergo development and are subject to various influences; they are differently interpreted and handed on in respectively different connections. Orthodox textbooks of patristics, which extend the time of the church fathers well into the present and contain chapters about the fathers of the twentieth century, indicate the relevance of the problem. In Greek patristics, one can find only relatively late efforts to present Christian knowledge systematically. There are also no such efforts in Russian literature before the fifteenth century. In addition, and in connection with it, the term "theology" has a different meaning than in the West so that one should rather speak, with regard to the epoch of the Rus', of "theological literature."

The Rus' had to receive all its theological literature from Byzantium. This means that the first works were almost exclusively translations. It is estimated that about 90 percent of the circulated manuscripts were translations.[1] But regarding anonymous writings, it is often not clear whether they are original works or translations. Among original works, there were, above all, the chronicles and vitas[2] as well as (often stylized) sermon literature. But there is no speculative theological literature. There had to be, of course, first the formation of something like a theological culture, a climate in which theology could be pursued. Moreover, monks, as the primary agents of proper legal form, tended to preserve what was handed on but not to develop something creatively new.

The reception of Christianity and its theology from the imperial city also meant the reception of the contents and models of thinking that circulated there. The tenth century was a period when — after the epoch of Patriarch Photius — anti-Latin polemics was a propagated genre. The iconoclastic controversy, ending about 150 years before the Christianization of the Rus', made the icons and their theology part of the core of Orthodox identity. The developments in Christology after the Council of Chalcedon (451) attributed much greater importance to the divine nature of Jesus Christ than to his human one. Theology obtained a strong mystical trend through the significance of monasticism in Byzantium. These, then, were the conditions under which early Russian authors created their works.

Especially characteristic for the Old Russian literature is the almost total absence of any secular literature. The old Russian theological and ecclesiastical literature is extensively identical with literature altogether, if one disregards, above all, the famous *Tale of Igor's Campaign*, a profane heroic poem. In Byzantium, on the other hand, a secular literature had

---

1. Gerhard Podskalsky, *Christentum und theologische Literatur in der Kiever Rus'* *(988-1237)* (Munich: C. H. Beck, 1982), 246.

2. Biographical sketches of monks.

developed. But, above all, the entire legacy of Greek antiquity existed there. The Byzantine Christian authors were taught by pagan philosophers and writers. This was not the case in the Rus', except in some writings of metropolitans or theologians who came from Greece. Moreover, the first specifically national characteristics need to be registered for the Rus', especially in the interpretation of history and of lives of saints. They are the consequence of totally different situations in which the Rus' and the Byzantine Empire existed. In addition, there is again and again another specification in the literature, namely, the efforts against the "double faith," the remnants of paganism.

Old Russian literature consists of sermons, canonical writings, and works of church history in the broader sense, that is, besides chronicles, above all, hagiography. There are almost no dogmatic and exegetical works. Biographical material about authors is nearly totally missing. The later metropolitan Ilarion (eleventh century) is the most important author of sermon literature; his "Sermon on Law and Grace," a praise of Saint Vladimir, contributed decisively to the canonization of the first Christian prince of the Rus'. It represents one of the most important works of Old Russian literature as a whole.

Most of the literature originated in the monasteries. In time, there also originated ecclesiastical and theological writings that dealt with questions of "events of the day." They indicated not only a reception but also the beginnings of independent literary work among the Eastern Slavs. There also were polemical writings that were frequently directed against the Catholic Church. Although the schism of 1054 had not shown any immediate consequences in the Russian Church, there already existed an anti-Latin trend in Byzantium. The political efforts of the Catholic Church to influence the Rus', as well as the military efforts of Western powers, contributed to an even stronger development of this genre. So the skepticism of the Russian Church toward Western influences also had a foundation in theology.

A series of names of authors is handed on from the first centuries of the Christian Rus', but there is no great, significant theologian who might have created a school. This has to do with the restraint toward dogmatic topics. The theology of the time was comprehensive, preserving, and continued with what it had received, without delivering new designs. But it laid the foundation for future developments, which in the later Russian history of theology were always situated between the preservation of what was traditional and the integration of what was new.

Western Influence

The Greek influence decreased also with the fall of Constantinople; it was understood as a strange influence. At the same time, Western thinking gradually gained entry in Russia, above all, through Kiev. There were Orthodox believers in greater numbers in the Polish-Lithuanian state, with roots in the southwestern center of the Rus'. They helped the Orthodox Church to borrow, in various ways, ideas from the Western denominations, above all, with the intention of being better armed against their arguments. The Orthodox nobility needed to pass through the Catholic educational institutions in order to become an integral part in the elite of the state since the legislation often favored Catholics. This meant the danger of conversion and with it a decay of education in the Orthodoxy of Poland-Lithuania. Consequently, the hierarchy took great pains to create Orthodox possibilities for education. This happened, on the one hand, in many cities through the Orthodox lay-brotherhoods that were very engaged with this question and, on the other hand, through diocesan schools that were gradually established, but above all through Kiev College.

For these reasons, one finds some important Orthodox theologians educated at Catholic institutions in Poland-Lithuania, mostly at Jesuit colleges, or sent to Rome for study. During their education they were Catholic, but they reconverted to Orthodoxy after returning to their homeland. Now, as experts in Catholic theology, they were in a position to supply systematic foundations for Orthodox theology. This happened often by borrowing from scholasticism, in whose spirit they had been schooled. Since the Reformed theology in Poland was quite influential and attracted many of the Orthodox, especially members of the elite, the ways of argumentation developed in the Counter-Reformation, mediated through the Catholic education, could well be used against it. When some of these Orthodox theologians, so schooled, later reached Russia, they influenced not only the theology of Russian Orthodoxy there, but also the ecclesiastical structure.

Peter Mogila (1596-1647) was probably the most important theologian to whom many of these assertions apply. He came from Moldavian nobility and in 1627 became archimandrite of the Cave Monastery after studies in Poland where the Counter-Reformation had made its mark. Orthodoxy in Poland was severely weakened through the Union of Brest and also through Reformed convictions to which the Ukrainian nobility adhered. Mogila intended to procure new strength for it and did so by borrowing from Western theology. He improved the education and publications of his church and finally became metropolitan of Kiev in 1633. A year earlier, he had established a new school in the Cave Monastery, Kiev College *(Collegium Kioviense)*. In 1694, when Kiev and a part of Ukraine belonged to Moscow, this institution was given the right to teach also theology, and it became the Kiev Academy in 1701. Mogila was canonized in 1996.

Mogila's chief work is his catechism, published in 1640 with the title *Orthodox Confession (Confessio Orthodoxa)*. Its title, which calls to mind the "confessional writings" of the Reformation, its form, and its publication in Latin furnish evidence for Western influences. The catechism was written under the influence of Petrus Canisius, and Mogila borrowed material from Catholic teaching regarding controversial Catholic-Orthodox questions. Regarding the question of the moment of the transubstantiation, he settled for the Words of Institution (instead of the *epiclesis*); baptism must not be done by immersion, as was customary in Ukraine anyway; and regarding the question of the location of purification, he moved closer to the Catholic doctrine of purgatory. The catechism was translated into Greek (available today) without these Catholic elements. The authorities of the Greek Church and also a synod in Constantinople accepted it in 1643. Mogila strongly marked Orthodoxy with his confession, but he also took it into Western forms of thinking. This methodical acceptance seemed necessary to him in the situation of his time and in the Polish-Lithuanian context. The blame for a "pseudomorphosis"[3] did not appear until the twentieth century. This means that the Western form also had consequences for the contents and, therefore, changed Orthodox theology in its essence.

In the time of Peter, theology was in strong measure marked by justifying the decisions of the tsar. Here, too, there was borrowing from the West, which was not surprising. For, on the one hand, the two leading theologians, Stefan Yavorskiy and Feofan Prokopovich, came from Kiev and had enjoyed a Catholic education, and on the other hand, the West counted as a model anyway. The baroque style, otherwise not known in Orthodoxy, was accepted and also affected theological literature. The

---

3. So Georges Florovsky, "Westliche Einflüsse in der russischen Theologie," in *Proces-Verbaux du premier congres de Theologie orthodoxe a Athenes,* ed. Hamlikar S. Alivisatos (Athens: Pyrsos, 1939), 222.

disputed writing of Yavorskiy, "Rock of Faith," had the general title "Rock of Faith, to the Sons of the Holy, Orthodox-Catholic Church for Strengthening and Spiritual Edification; but to Those Who Are Offended by the Stumbling Block and Scandal for Openness and Improvement," showing the baroque influence on the Russian language.

It was of great significance for the continuation of Russian theology that there was no university theology. Even after the establishment of universities, theology had no place there. This was a momentous development for theological scholarship because it did not have to maintain itself in concert with "university study" *(universitas litterarum)* and remained isolated from the intellectual trends in the country. Fundamentally, this exclusion of theology from the sciences continued in the Soviet Union because then, too, theology could only be taught at ecclesiastical institutions, and theological research had hardly any contact with other disciplines. Still today, one can observe the phenomenon that many intellectuals, who are close to the church, and also a number of priests, originally had another education, quite often in the natural sciences, before they turned to theology. Occasionally, this leads to conflicts with those theologians who defend themselves against new and continuing developments.

In the beginnings of the Rus', there were schools at monasteries that were used only for the education of their own recruits and the secular nobility. Even afterward, predominantly monks, but also bishops, were responsible for theological work. There was no theological education, above all, for the "white clergy," the parish clergy. In 1685, a school was established in Moscow from which evolved the "Slavonic-Greek-Latin Academy." In 1754, it became an academy only for theological education (since 1812, it has been located in the Trinity Sergiy Monastery of Sergiyev Posad, about forty-four miles from Moscow). The "Spiritual Regulation" from the reign of Peter decreed that all dioceses had to establish seminaries for the education of the secular clergy. These institutions were not scientific-theological establishments, but they were to enable pupils (mostly sons of priests) to do parish ministry. In the beginning of the nineteenth century, theological academies were established in St. Petersburg, Moscow, Kiev, and Kazan'. They, too, were not connected with the public system of education, but they achieved a great reputation. The academies published journals that, for the time being, offered translations of many writings of the church fathers and of canons of councils, thus providing the basic theological texts in Russian. In the second half of the nineteenth century, systematic-theological writings increasingly appeared alongside ascetical ones. The system of academies remained until after the October Revolution, when the Bolsheviks made any systematic theological education impossible. All these reforms and changes in the system of theological education were produced by the initiative of the state, not by actions of the church. This, too, shows the great dependence of the church on the state.

The restricted situation of the church after the reforms of Peter led to a considerable emphasis of the realm of mysticism and of personal piety opposite to the institutionalized theology. Theology was viewed in close relationship with the church itself. One had no confidence that it would be able to produce innovative impulses for spiritual progress. The strong emphasis on reason since Peter, and especially under Catherine, also allowed influences that favored a transconfessional theology that engendered a certain de-confessionalization of Orthodoxy and, as a reaction against it, an even stronger insistence on what was customary.

In the nineteenth century, the Westernizing of Russian theology also continued in the academies. Only in 1840 was instruction in Latin finally abolished and it became customary to no longer comment on theological textbooks but to research the sources of the church, that is, Holy Scripture, the church fathers, and liturgy. That is why, above all, historical subjects, like church history itself, the study of sources, and liturgiology became very important. Many manuscripts were edited, among them many liturgical sources. Some theologians had studied at universities in western Europe so that Western literature was known and used. The emphasis on church history led to a sharpening of consciousness for earlier epochs and developments of the church. Consequently, knowledge of something like the importance of the patriarchy became real; it then was used after the nineteenth century in the discussions about its reintroduction. But the desolate situation of the church and of theology prevented an independent theological development that could have taken hold in broad circles of theologians. This was rather the case in religious philosophy, which was, of course, ecclesiastically marked but not so much under the direct control of the church.

Some of the more important theologians of modern times should be mentioned: first of all, Metropolitan Platon (Levshin) of Moscow (1737-1812). He studied at the Moscow Academy and became archimandrite of the famous Trinity Sergiy Monastery in Sergiyev Posad. Catherine, who became aware of him, made him the tutor of the later tsar Pavel I. Platon published an "orthodox dogmatics" in his honor, the first systematic presentation of theology in Russian. It was often translated (into German in 1770) and had great influence on later Russian catechisms. Platon, who became metropolitan of Moscow in 1787, also published a two-volume church history, which likewise was the first attempt of a comprehensive presentation. In his presentation of Orthodox doctrine, Platon remains entangled in the structures that had determined the theology of his time through the Western alignment. But in his position as rector of the Moscow Academy, Platon refused to call instructors from Kiev — a sign of the slowly growing consciousness that it was necessary to concentrate on one's own tradition.

The first important church historian also was a bishop, and worked not only in the historical field but also in the systematic one. The dogmatic work of Metropolitan Makariy (Bulgakov, 1816-82) was strongly marked by the West and, despite intensive criticism, had at first no little influence, but became less important later. His twelve-volume Russian church history is uncritical over long periods, even when it refers to sources. But the author tried to let a historical-critical method have its way. Makariy even risked a conflict with the synod over it. Although his church history can no longer measure up to the present norms, it is still an important testimony of the beginnings of scientific history in Russia.

The antagonist of Metropolitan Makariy was a layman, Yevgeniy Golubinskiy (1834-1912), who was professor of church history at the Moscow Theological Academy. He published the first strictly source-critical church history that traced in four volumes the development of the Russian Church until well into the sixteenth century.

Finally, there is Vasiliy Bolotov (1854-1900), also a professor of church history. He became famous because he was occupied with the question of the *filioque*.[4] Since he was secretary of a synodical commission for dialogue with the Old Catholic Church, he worked with this topic. He became convinced that this addition in the Nicene Creed had no church-dividing character but characterized a Western theological opinion. Bolotov's works about Origen are also significant; they investigate and rediscover, above all, the doctrine of the Trinity of this church father who, as a "heretic," is never especially appreciated in Orthodoxy.

These few names may suffice to provide an insight into the theology

---

4. The doctrine that the Holy Spirit proceeds from the Father "and the Son" (*filioque* in Latin) rather than from the Father alone.

of the nineteenth century. It was later identified as "school theology," meaning, above all, that it was sufficient for the pragmatic demands of a basic theological education but did not exhibit any strength for creative new beginnings and especially no inclination to return to the patristic foundations of Orthodox theology. Such a renaissance was to come only in the midst of the twentieth century, brought about because of the historical circumstances in Russian history. Besides, the blame of "school theology" involved not only Russian theology but was aimed at Orthodoxy in general, that is, also in Greece and in other countries.

Philosophy of Religion in the Nineteenth Century

Whereas theology was confined to the narrow ecclesiastical realm and was also subject to ecclesiastical censorship, nontheologians who were interested in religion could ponder theological questions, although they could not always avoid public censorship. That is why some of the important works of the time appeared first abroad and only later in Russia, sometimes long after the author's death. In the Russia of the nineteenth century, a significant philosophy of religion developed that also had enduring consequences for theology. A general interest in religious questions, also, for example, by famous literary figures (Dostoyevskiy, Tolstoy), created a climate for the treatment of such topics.

In the wake of the Napoleonic Wars at the beginning of the nineteenth century, Russian troops were, for the first time, in western Europe and so also came into contact with "the West." Earlier, Western thinking had already reached Russia despite the strong censorship under the enlightened rulers. After the failure of their revolt during a change of sovereigns in 1825, the so-called Dekabrists were severely punished. Many young noblemen were exiled to Siberia. This situation created an intellectual vacuum. Attempts were made to fill it with ideas borrowed from Europe. This created two alignments that became decisive for the Russian philosophy of the nineteenth century, the so-called Slavophiles (*slavyanofily*) and the Westernizers (*zapadniki*). In these two alignments, the old question of Russia's orientation was manifested anew, namely, how Russia should conduct itself toward Western influences. The increasing contacts with the West had made the question virulent. But no consideration was given to the fact that the alignment with a critical attitude to the West was also, for its part, under Western influence and was based on

Western models of thought. Moreover, such a phenomenon was also not new in the Russian history of ideas. It is really not possible to draw a narrow line between the two alignments since the ideas have frequently been used incorrectly; many intellectuals also disclose initial stages that could be attributed to either side.

The Slavophiles, who had a greater impact and, therefore, shall be presented here in detail, were strongly influenced by romanticism and German idealism. The appeal to the Russian people, to old Russian, Slavic (hence the designation) values and the question of Russia's destiny, played a central role for them. According to their worldview, a tendency developed in the western European culture that departed more and more from the old and correct Christian principles. The reason for this was the overemphasis on the human being in the Western history of ideas, shown in such phenomena as humanism, the Enlightenment, and rationalism. So the true relation to God came up short, and there was talk about a "spiritual Nestorianism"; just as Nestorius attributed too much importance to the human nature of Christ in the fifth century, so Western thinking accentuated too much the human being. The result was an individualization in which human community had no longer any significance. This is extremely so in Protestantism where the individual Christian is completely without any ties because of a total lack of any obligation. But this problem of the Christian West is also evident in Catholicism, where the individual element completely vanishes in favor of the absolute authority of the papacy.

The Orthodox counterbalance, therefore, consists in the community and is realized as ecclesiastical community in Orthodoxy. The Slav does not know individualism but is a being in community that does not relinquish its true destiny by entering this community but finds it only there. Here, Slavic forms of living together, especially the rural village, are strongly idealized. The ecclesiastical community is also not a relinquishing of the identity of the individual but its fulfillment. The later-developed word "Sobornost" (in Russian: *sobornost'*) is the central category of this conception. The term can hardly be translated into another language and, because of its origin, connotes terms like "conciliarity" (from "council") or "synodality" (from "synod") as well as "catholicity." In the ecclesiastical realm, it means the conviction of the whole church to cooperate in important decisions and also in the search for truth. The most significant theorist of Sobornost, Alexey Khomyakov (1804-60), an aristocratic physician and historian, even developed the thesis that decisions of councils only gain validity when they are accepted by the entire church. The "Robber Synods" of the ancient church, but also the Union Councils of the Middle Ages that were not accepted by the East, are evidence for his conviction.

Sobornost implies a transindividual ecclesiastical consciousness into which the consciousness of the individual believer is inserted. The categories of unity, mutual love, and freedom are ideally realized in this Orthodox conception. But in the Western denominations, unity (Catholicism) and freedom (Protestantism) are so strongly overemphasized that Christian love disappears and the balance between the elements is disturbed. In his writings, Khomyakov is very sharply and polemically anti-Western; like all Slavophiles, he offers a highly negative interpretation of the reforms of Peter I.

It becomes evident that the classic idea of the church no longer played a special role in Sobornost's emphasis of the community of all in the church. The Slavophiles had a great interest in ecclesiastical questions since they thought of the church only as Orthodox. But they were interested in the community of Sobornost, not in the hierarchy or ecclesiastical structure. This perspective of community also determines the interpretation of questions about ecclesiastical authority and about the power to make decisions. Consequently, decisions of the hierarchy in councils have always only relative character and must be confirmed by the church at large through acceptance (or nonacceptance). It is not surprising that Khomyakov could not publish his writings during his lifetime in Russia — they did not pass the censorship. They appeared first in French in Paris; a Russian edition was arranged in Moscow only after his death.

The conception of Sobornost had far-reaching consequences. The discussions at the local council of 1917 were marked by it. The introduction of the patriarchate was opposed by the argument that it would be detrimental to Sobornost, and because of these convictions the patriarch was given only very limited authority. There was, to be sure, also resistance against this thesis in Orthodoxy, above all in the Greek version. But today, not a few theologians are representatives of Sobornost theory, some in a modified form. That is also mitigated by the fact that there is no explicitly defined content for Sobornost but that it means different things. But it exposed the emphasis on the meaning of reception for ecclesiastical life. The emphasis of the role of the people of God also gained significance in the Catholic theology of the twentieth century via the detour of the Russian emigration in Paris and its contact with French theology (here, above all, the Dominican Yves Congar must be mentioned), until well into the Second Vatican Council. So the Catholic discussion of the topic "reception" in recent decades can be indirectly traced to this stance of Russian theology.

It should be noted, for the sake of completeness, that reference is also made today to Sobornost (in its aforementioned vagueness) in the secular realm of Russia. In efforts to emphasize the unity of the Russian nation, one has recourse to this term and understands it in the sense of unity and community, or national unity.

Accordingly, the vision of the Slavophiles points to a special task and mission of Russia for Christianity as a whole. Since the Western churches had lost their roots, they should turn to Orthodoxy, because the salvation of Europe and the Western church is only in Russia. This is the thesis of the philosopher Konstantin Leontyev (1831-91), for whom the category of aesthetics played a special role. He saw it realized in Russian autocracy as well as in the lives of simple folk, in contrast to Western, especially democratic, models. Slavophiles also developed far-reaching cultural philosophical ideas, relating, for example, to Islam or to Russia as a European and Asian country. Finally, mysticism was significant for them since Orthodoxy was perceived as "transrational."

The most important philosopher of the Slavophiles was Vladimir Solovyev (1853-1900). With regard to theology, above all, his "Sophiology" (the doctrine of divine wisdom) is important. He understands the wisdom of God that not only has an Old Testament background but also is frequently thought of hypostatically, as it were, in Orthodoxy (visible, for example, in the dedication of the Hagia Sophia Cathedral in Constantinople, of Saint Sophia's Cathedral in Kiev, and of churches in other Russian cities) as an all-encompassing principle of sustaining the world. On the basis of his own visions, he saw "wisdom" *(sophia)* personified as a woman. He strongly influenced subsequent theologians, above all, Sergiy Bulgakov and Pavel Florenskiy, who developed these ideas further.

The idea of a universal unity is central for Solovyev. Just as divinity and humanity are united in Jesus Christ, so also one must strive for the unification of religion and science, as well as of East and West. With regard to the church, this means the unity of Latin and Greek Christianity under the pope. Solovyev consistently applied this idea by receiving Holy Communion from a Catholic priest; this act was frequently viewed by

Catholic authors as a conversion. But, as a matter of fact, he remained Orthodox, or, more precisely, regarded, at least for himself, the schism of the churches as overcome.

We conclude with the opposing philosophical movement, the Westernizers. Their background is more French than German philosophy, especially utopianism. Since they saw a salvation for Russia only in Western thought, they had no great interest in ecclesiastical questions and also did not produce any representatives who might have put their stamp on theological thinking. Some Orthodox believers converted to the Catholic Church. But neither they nor the Anglican Church, in which there was more and more interest because of close proximity to Russia with regard to contents, exercised any great influence. Many representatives of the Western-oriented philosophy became radical and created the foundation for Russian anarchism and for the various socialist and communist trends that were to determine the political life of the late nineteenth and early twentieth centuries.

Theological Departures in the Twentieth Century

The time after the revolution had a dramatic effect on theology and connected it in a new way with Western theology. But it also made it aware of its Eastern roots. In Russia itself, theological work was hardly still possible. The closing of educational institutions, the prohibition of all publications, and the forced discontinuation of all contacts with churches abroad made the work de facto impossible, which was already intimated by the beginnings of the persecution of the church. After World War II, the church was able to publish the series "Theological Works." In it appeared, above all, shorter drafts of qualification papers from the theological academies in Leningrad and Zagorsk — the name of Sergiyev Posad appeared during the Soviet time. But no textbooks could be published, and no theology could be found outside the academies.

A significant theologian, who became a victim of the regime, was the priest Pavel Florenskiy (1882-1937). Originally, he was a natural scientist, then he studied theology, and because of his expertise in natural science, was first tolerated and even could, until 1933, work in a public research institution, where he drew attention to himself by always wearing priestly vestments. He was exiled to a camp where he still was devoted to scientific work, as shown in his notes and letters. In 1937 he was shot to death in the camp. He was a "nonperson" in the Soviet Union, and for a while, some of his works were published secretly; since 1977, they have also sporadically appeared in ecclesiastical journals. Since the 1980s, he has experienced a renaissance and today is known as one of the most important and most significant theologians who also influenced Greek, Romanian, and Serbian theologians. Some of his works have been translated into English.

Florenskiy's chief work originated in 1914 under the title *The Pillar and Foundation of Truth: An Attempt of an Orthodox Theodicy in Twelve Letters.* It is an attempt to present the doctrine of the Trinity from a mystical perspective, based on the Orthodox tradition. The influence of the philosophy of religion, especially through Solovyev, is unmistakable. The mystical aspect emphasizes the category of experience, so central for Florenskiy. In a sharply anti-Western critique, Florenskiy disputes the right of Western theologians to understand any Orthodox theology. They remind him of classes ("in the West") that reportedly claim that one can learn how to swim on dry land. Florenskiy also explains Sophiology by likening it to a person who participates in the life of the Trinity but simultaneously manifests it in human life. He produced other works on the theology of icons, again sharply criticizing Western religious painting.

In the first years of the Soviet period, many theologians went abroad, be it through emigration or expulsion. There they tried to expand Russian theological thinking. It is open to question to what extent these theologians can still be linked to Russian theology. There is no doubt perhaps regarding the best-known and most important exile theologian, Sergiy Bulgakov (1871-1944). He came from a family of priests and began training at a seminary. But then he totally rejected the church and studied economics. As a professor, first in Kiev and then in Moscow, he was aligned with Marxism. But soon, he again turned to religion and became occupied with philosophy of religion. The title of his collection of essays, *From Marxism to Idealism,* elucidates this development. In 1917, he participated as a delegate in the local council and then was briefly a coworker of Patriarch Tikhon (Belavin). In 1918, he was ordained as a priest. But in 1923 the Soviet government deprived him of his citizenship. He went to Paris and became the first dean and professor of dogmatics at the newly established Institute Saint-Serge. He occupied both positions until his death.

Bulgakov offered a synoptic dogmatic presentation in two extensive trilogies. The first, and smaller one, deals with the Mother of God, John the Baptist, and the angels. It is a theological approach to the Deesis Icon that depicts Mary and John the Baptist praying before Jesus. Here, Sophiology plays an important role. The second trilogy is occupied with Christology, pneumatology, and ecclesiology (including eschatology).

Bulgakov's work is clearly defined by his presentation of Sophia. To him, the divine wisdom is an expression of the presence and activity of God in the world. But it belongs to the realm of divine energies, and therefore is uncreated. In this way, a narrow relation is created between God and the divine creation, without abandoning the transcendence of God. Here, too, the idea of the universal unity becomes clear, which indeed had been moved to the foreground in the philosophy of religion. Bulgakov stresses this, above all, in his Christology; the entire second trilogy is titled *On the God-Humanity.*

With this way of speaking of divine energies, Bulgakov takes up the notions of the Greek theologian Gregorios Palamas (d. 1359), and therefore can be considered one of the forerunners of neo-Palamism, which gained great significance in the Orthodox theology of the twentieth century. Bulgakov's doctrine of Sophia was condemned by the Russian Church abroad in 1927 and by the church in Moscow in 1935. But the metropolitan in Paris stood by him so that he could keep his professorship.

Bulgakov was also very active ecumenically. He participated at the large conferences before the establishment of the World Council of Churches in Lausanne in 1927, as well as in Edinburgh and Oxford in 1937, and he was a leader in the famous brotherhood of "St. Alban and St. Sergius." He also wrote an introduction to the theological thought in Orthodoxy for Western readers.

The American Russian theologian of Russian descent, Georges Florovsky (Georgiy Florovskiy, 1893-1979), resided abroad after 1920, mostly in Paris until 1948, then in New York, Boston (at Harvard), and Princeton. He was an instructor of patristics in Saint-Serge, then briefly the successor of Bulgakov as dogmatician, and subsequently church historian in the USA; in addition, he was a member of the Central Committee of the World Council of Churches for many years. Florovsky had an effect on Orthodoxy that can hardly be overestimated, namely, he tried to bring it back to its patristic roots. His lecture at the first Congress of Orthodox Theologians in Athens in 1936 exposed the "pseudomorphosis" of theology and demanded a return to the Fathers.[5] The first reaction, delayed by

5. See above, n. 3.

World War II, was an affirmation of the importance of Gregorios Palamas so that neo-Palamism became an important direction of thinking in Orthodoxy today. In addition, there emerged a reconsideration of patristic theology, not only in terms of content but also, above all, with a quest for the ways in which Orthodox theology had been entangled for centuries. The most important consequence of this change was a new emphasis on liturgy as a theological source and development, respectively, redevelopment of a eucharistic ecclesiology. Theologians of the Russian emigration, such as John Meyendorff (d. 1992), Alexander Schmemann (d. 1983), and Nicolas Afanasieff (d. 1966), are important representatives of the "neo-Platonic synthesis" demanded by Florovsky. However, this already was no longer a matter of Russian theology. Florovsky did not represent an absolute new beginning; already Florenskiy had showed that the contemporary form of the school theology was considered to be not genuine and that a reconsideration of the sources seemed to be necessary. It was Florovsky who realized this reconsideration.

Today, it is again possible to do theology in Russia without any limitation. But it will take some time, after the complete deforestation in the twentieth century, before a broad theological landscape is once again established. Hopeful beginnings are already visible. The works of many earlier authors, of exiled theologians, and of many Greek and other Orthodox theologians are translated. The number of institutional establishments can hardly be surveyed, and not all of them began with the blessing of the church. Moreover, they have different standards. The church sends some of its theologians to foreign countries, to Catholic as well as to Protestant faculties. It is, of course, also not surprising that the church itself, at the present time, views the qualification and education of theologians as a first priority.

It is to be expected that the search for a new identity and a new beginning will also become evident in theology, just as it characterizes many other realms of the Russian Church today. This process had already begun in the emigration. As often in the past, so also today, there is the question of how to deal with tradition and how to accept new elements that are sometimes older than what is seen as tradition. Already now, it is apparent that some phenomena are rejected only because they are "Western." But it is, indeed, the new theological stance of theology from the "West" that can lead Orthodox theology back to its roots despite all the difficulties this may, at times, cause for the Western churches and for ecumenical dialogue. The great theologians, such as Bulgakov and

Florovsky, prove through their work that authentic Orthodoxy and ecumenical engagement do not exclude each other. But it will take some time before it becomes clear in which direction Russian Orthodox theology will go, or whether there is only one direction.

CHAPTER SEVEN

Monasticism

M onasticism originated in the Christian East, and Western monasticism received its marks from there. Still today, monasticism is an
institution of great significance in the churches of the East. The "holy
mountain" Athos is considered the center of Orthodox monasticism and
represents a unique institution of ascetic and consecrated life. In Orthodoxy, bishops are always chosen from the monks; that is why secular
priests, who are usually married, have no access to the highest ecclesiastical ranks. Unlike the West, the Christian East knows no orders. Monks
and nuns live according to the rules of Saint Basileios (d. 379), as well as
according to the prescriptions of their respective monasteries. The monasteries are subject to the respective bishop and thus are not exempt from
the jurisdiction of the bishops, as they are in the West. The so-called
Stauropegial monasteries are subject directly to the patriarch, that is, to
the head of the church.

Already in the ancient church, two forms of monastic life can be distinguished: being a hermit or living in the monastery. Hermits live
"idiorhythmically," that is, according to their own rhythm, sometimes in
loose associations or colonies, but with their own housing and daily
schedule. It is important for monasteries to have demarcated space, an
area enclosed by walls, the common daily schedule with prayer, work,
food, and rest, as well as subordination to an abbot. There, one lives
"cenobitically," in community. Both phenomena can be found in Russian
church history: opposite to the monasteries, established by noble donors
(ktitors) in the cities, are the hermitages that originated in solitude, motivated by the need to retreat from the world. Reference was already made

to the important role of monks in the opening up of space, and the Startsy, living in retreat, fulfilled an important role, above all, in the nineteenth century in Russian society.

Three monastic waves can be distinguished in Russian church history. (1) After the Christianization of the Rus', numerous monasteries were quickly established. In 1240, at the time of the conquest of Kiev, there were already more than a hundred convents. Since they were located, above all, in the south, monastic life declined with the invasion of the Tartars. (2) In the fourteenth century, monastic life was linked to the name of Sergiy of Radonezh, the founder of a monastery named after him, the Trinity Sergiy Monastery in Sergiyev Posad, near Moscow; he also established many other monasteries with cenobitic rules. Many of his disciples founded other monasteries. In the fifteenth century, the tension between monastic asceticism in solitude and the influence of monasticism in the world caused a quarrel that was finally solved in favor of the latter stance. (3) After the restrictions of monastic life through the reforms of Peter in the eighteenth and nineteenth centuries, the mystical aspect of monastic life began to play a significant role. It was expressed, above all, in the activity of the Startsy. After the revolution of 1917, monasteries were, from the very outset, in the center of the persecutions. After World War II, there were many monasteries in the territory occupied by the German army; they were gradually closed in subsequent years, above all, at the end of the 1950s in connection with de-Stalinization. Only after the end of the Soviet Union were many new monasteries again established. This development can be clearly recognized in the statistics.[1]

Year	Monasteries (Men)	Convents (Women)
1701	965	236
1810	358	94

1. See Igor Smolitsch, *Russisches Mönchtum. Entstehung, Entwicklung und Wesen 988-1917* (Würzburg: Augustinus Verlag, 1953), 538. For 1945, 1968, 1960, and 1961, see Jane Ellis, *The Russian Orthodox Church: A Contemporary History* (London and Sydney: Croom Helm, 1986), 125. For 1974, see Peter Hauptmann and Gerd Stricker, eds., *Die Orthodoxe Kirche in Russland. Dokumente ihrer Geschichte (860-1980)* (Göttingen: Vandenhoeck & Ruprecht, 1988), 890. For 2007, see http://www.patriarchia.ru/db/text/1402889.html (accessed August 6, 2012). There were only two monasteries in the territory of the Russian Soviet Republic in the latter days of the USSR; the rest were in other republics.

1914	550	475
1935	0	0
1945		104
1958		69
1961		40
1974	3	13
1987	7	13
2010	398	407

The Kiev Cave Monastery

The most important, though perhaps not the oldest, monastery of the Kievan Rus' is the Kiev Cave Monastery, which was established in the middle of the eleventh century and represented for more than two centuries the center of Christian life. It is located on the high bank above the Dnepr and is still today most impressive with its monumental structures and long subterranean passages and chapels. It is surmised that it originated at an earlier, pre-Christian cult site.

According to reports from chronicles, it was founded by a monk named Antoniy who was said to have come from Mount Athos.[2] Having the same name as the father of Christian monasticism, Saint Anthony the Great, may be coincidental, but it can also point to a typifying figure. It is clear, in any case, that Russian monasticism, like all of Russian Christendom, must have been initiated from Constantinople because there are no other models available from the past. It is equally clear that it was not founded by a prince. Antoniy was said to have lived in a cave he constructed himself at the bank of the Dnepr, and quickly other monks were said to have joined him.

The first abbot of the Cave Monastery was probably Feodosiy (d. 1074), who can be considered the real founder. In 1062, the first buildings were constructed above ground while he was in charge, among them a church that was soon supplanted by the Dormition [Assumption] of Mary Cathedral, built of stone and finished in 1075. The caverns, which were first probably used, above all, for ascetic purposes, were also expanded in time and

2. According to Nestor's Chronicle, with the report about the foundation of the Cave Monastery, in Samuel Hazzard Cross and Olgerd P. Sherbowitz-Wetzor, *The Russian Primary Chronicle* (Cambridge, Mass.: Medieval Academy of America, 1953), 139-42.

linked with each other through passages. Today, there are 180 under-ground caverns as well as several hundred forty-inch passages. The caverns are no longer inhabited, but relics of saints are stored there; many serve as chapels.

Feodosiy introduced the rules of the renowned Studios Monastery in Constantinople; they were accepted in the entire world of Orthodoxy. They spread from the Cave Monastery to all Russian monasteries. The monks, above all, the abbots, served as advisers, but also as admonishers of the grand princes. There were several conflicts between the princes and the Cave Monastery. They also advised the metropolitans, whose successors often were monks of the Cave Monastery. Otherwise, prayer and manual labor were the most important activities of the monks, simi-lar to the monks of the ancient church. Feodosiy set a high value on a modest style of life and on support of the needy; he institutionalized tasks of the monastery by constructing an almshouse and a hospital.

Monks became important as authors of chronicles (of the early Rus-sian literature altogether). Although Nestor's Chronicle is, to be sure, not a reliable document, it is the most important source for the early history of the Russian Church. It portrays the beginnings of the Russian Church, of-ten with an apologetic or transfigured purpose, but with much indispens-able information. The *Paterikon* ("Book of the Fathers") from the thir-teenth century is a collection of stories about the first twenty-four monks of the Cave Monastery. It depicts the ascetic life of the monks, manifested, for example, by the fact that they did not leave their cavern for a long time, or never left it, and their battle with demons. The collection portrays the monastery as a center of monastic asceticism in a corrupted world.

The Cave Monastery was a place of uninterrupted monastic life from its beginnings until the twentieth century. When Kiev was Lithuanian, and later, Polish, the monastery functioned as a bastion of Orthodoxy. But the Western theological influences still reached Russia via Kiev, and thus via the Cave Monastery, especially since the Kiev Academy was lo-cated there in its first years. In the sixteenth and seventeenth centuries, it was the center of the opposition to the Union. Stefan Yavorskiy as well as Feofan Prokopovich exemplify two abbots who were later brought to Russia and there exercised a great influence over the Russian Church.

In 1927, the Cave Monastery was dissolved by the Communist regime and served as a museum. In 1946, it was reopened as a monastery in the wake of the concessions to the church. Under Khrushchev, it was again dissolved in 1960, but then was returned to the church in the *perestroika* and in connection with the millennial celebration of 1988. In the complicated ecclesiastical landscape of today's Ukraine, it belongs to the church of the Moscow Patriarchate.

The Dispute about Monastic Property

The monasteries of the Rus' were first mostly endowments. In time, they acquired property and frequently became very wealthy. But wealth did not suit the ascetic demands of monasticism. The process of colonization through hermits, described in connection with the expansion of Christianity, entailed that the monasteries, involved in it, also became wealthy through economic stabilization or through endowments and legacies. That removed them from the ideal of asceticism. This was frequently a topic of dispute within monasticism, above all, when the question of the beginnings was raised. The increasing wealth of the monasteries also became the subject of disputes with the state, which wanted to acquire them, including not only land but especially the peasants settled on it. The increase of ascetic impulses in the fourteenth century made the question of the relationship between asceticism and monastic wealth more virulent. But one can find next to the increased withdrawal from the world and the search for solitude also Sergiy of Radonezh, who reformed monasticism by emphasizing the cenobitic aspect in the monastery he founded in 1337. The dispute between two trends escalated in the fifteenth century (at the end of which, one-third of the land was monastic property!). Nil Sorskiy and Joseph of Volokolamsk were the spokesmen of the two sides.

Nil, born in 1433, became a disciple of the "Hesychasts" ("adherents of stillness" in Greek), a theological orientation according to which a monk was to concentrate his life on asceticism in order to attain a vision of God. He was a monk in the Kirill Monastery at White Lake in the north of the country. It had been founded by a disciple of Sergiy of Radonezh. Nil moved from there to the river Sora, from which he received his surname. He and several like-minded companions founded a hermitage. In this form of communal life, the spiritual father (*starets* in Russian, "old man," "old monk") had an important spiritual authority in the group. It was different from the classic anchorites who put more emphasis on life in complete solitude. There was, to be sure, also a strict asceticism in the hermitage. But it was a voluntary subordination under a monk who was accepted as a model. Moreover, obedience, so significant for cenobites, was not a central category for Nil. Rather, it was more a relationship of trust than of subordination. The "skit," as this kind of monastery was called, was not to have any property, not even valuables for the liturgy. The monastery also did not seek any relation to the state but was rather after distance from the world. The disciples of Nil were called "the nonpossessors," or, according to their geographical site, "the Trans-Volga Startsy."

Joseph was born in 1439-40 and became the founding abbot of the rich Volokolamsk Monastery, located about ninety miles northwest of Moscow. There was a strictly regulated relation between the monks and the abbot. The relation was marked by respect and obedience. The monastery was meant to be an institution that, to be sure, considerably limited the freedom of the monks but in return procured salvation for them. Part of such logic was the education of the monks. For monasteries, indeed, fulfilled a task for the state since there was always a need for bishops to be well educated. Joseph insisted that the monasteries have property. On the one hand, property offered provision for the monks, and on the other hand, the church had to have an economic base in order to be taken seriously by the state as a partner. His disciples were called "Josephites."

It is clear that the two concepts strongly contradict each other, even though there were certainly common interests. For Nil, the salvation of the individual was in the foreground; for Joseph, it could be attained in a group. So in Russia, too, the old opposition arose between the individual monk, the hermit, and monks living in a cloister. This opposition is known from the history of the ancient church and already is alluded to in the old Russian chronicles.

In 1503, a synod met in Moscow where the viewpoint of Joseph prevailed. In the background, there are also disputes with heretics and conflicts about successions to the throne. Grand Prince Ivan III had to rely on the support of the church. He could not, without further ado, as he had intended, seize church property. Although the decision of the Moscow synod did not make strict asceticism disappear, it let it become a personal matter. This was to be so for a long time. Other reform movements were even qualified as sects. But Joseph, who had gained acceptance, joined the side of the grand prince without any reservations. Despite all later attempts of the state to seize church property, the decision meant that the respective ruler was to have an unrestricted supporter in the church, albeit one that was materially extremely powerful.

The concentration on the bishops (and thus also on the monks), as well as on the grand prince in the worldly realm, made it possible for the hierarchy in Russia always to play an important role. Reform movements hardly succeeded and were pushed to the realm of the sects. Monks, who were dissatisfied with the situation in the church, tended to seek solitude and to avoid being too close to the hierarchy and to ecclesiastical structures. Movements like the Western mendicant orders did not originate here; they might have been able to canalize such notions in the church.

The church was isolated in this phase of church history, and western European developments, such as humanism, were not accepted in Russia. So the church retained a closed view of the world. The old calendar, which started the year in September and counted time since the creation of the world, is a symbolic expression of this situation. It meant, with reference to the church, that, in contrast to the West, there was no secularization of daily life but rather a "monastization" of the world. The world became a monastery so that the monastic ideals also became valid for people living in the world. "Pious Russians fashion their personal and family lives also in our time in the spirit of monastic rules."[3] This is exemplified by the liturgy with its long worship services; the hours of prayers, still used today in parishes; and the extremely strict rules for fasting of the Orthodox Church. The observance of monastic rules is viewed as an ascetic ideal for the laity living in the world. The Russian "Housekeeping Book" *(Domostroy)* of the sixteenth century demonstrates this in its individual instructions for religious life in families.

The Startsy

After the victory of the "Josephites," there were still both trends in Russian monasticism: the dominating one, characterized by its closeness to the state, powerful, with wealthy monasteries and political influence; and the ascetic one of the hermits, with its strong accent on perfection and separation from the world. There were always connections to Mount Athos, with its great Russian Panteleymon Monastery of 1169, as well as monks who lived as hermits. They always could be found in Russia itself. The tension between hierarchy and charisma was sometimes expressed

---

3. Metropolitan Pitirim of Volokolamsk and Jurjev, eds., *Die Russische Orthodoxe Kirche* (New York: de Gruyter, Evangelisches Verlagswerk, 1988), 184.

in concrete conflicts, but was frequently not at all manifested. In the old Russian tradition, the tension between both monastic types is shown in the fact that great monasteries were established as endowments by princes, whereas the chronicle emphasizes that the Cave Monastery was established through ascetic endeavors.

The schism of the Old Believers, as well as the reforms under Peter I and Catherine II, was very detrimental to Russian monasticism. The Old Believers were strongly supported by monasteries, and the patriarchal church lost many of them. Moreover, the mystical-eschatological trend of the Old Believers attracted many of the ascetics. The restrictions on entering a monastery under Peter I and the final confiscation of monastic property under Catherine II deprived the monasteries of much of their basis of existence. On the other hand, the state church system made it not very attractive to seek spiritual experiences within the official church so that the mystical trend became more and more popular.

These circumstances encouraged the development of the so-called Startsy among ascetic monks. The designation "Starets" refers usually to an older monk who has a special spiritual authority. The designation comes from the monastic realm where such monks frequently were father confessors for fellow brethren and spiritual directors for young monks. However, the position of the Starets is not related to a specific function (like that of the master of novices, or the spiritual director in the West) but to his charism. In the Greek tradition there is the analogous designation *geron* ("older person"). The phenomenon is already known in the monasticism of the ancient church.

The Startsy became important in the Russian Church after the end of the eighteenth century, and their influence was to some extent a countermovement to the crisis of institutionalized monasticism. Monasteries and hermitages were concentrated in a semicircle, beginning north of St. Petersburg and extending south of Kiev. The principle of obedience and subordination became important for the pastoral guidance granted the young monks by the Startsy. It enabled the Startsy in an ideal manner to allow for the spiritual progress of a monk in his spiritual development. This, too, was a patristic legacy; back then, as well as in Russia, the acknowledgment of the spiritual authority of a "desert father" was a central element of the ascetic life.

Above all, in the nineteenth century, some of the Startsy became known far beyond their monastery or hermitage. They were advisers of believers who turned to them and put up with long journeys to get to them. Beyond that, some of the Startsy kept up an exhaustive correspondence with laypeople for spiritual guidance. The Starets Zosima in Dostoyevskiy's *The Brothers Karamazov* is the best-known literary evidence of such a spiritual adviser; the figure has its origin in the Starets Amvrosiy (Grenkov). In the nineteenth century, the hermitage Optina Pustyn', south of Moscow, where this and many other important Startsy lived and worked, was visited by many people in search of advice.

The Startsy had an extensive influence on numerous areas of social and ecclesiastical life. Many people did not make an important decision without the approval (the "blessing") of their Starets. This development is certainly also a consequence of the weakness of the established church; most priests could hardly perform the functions of pastoral advice and care, above all, with the members of the intelligentsia. But many Startsy had a high degree of education, and some were bishops who had withdrawn from their office to the monastery or hermitage, so they could be adequate partners in dialogue with those seeking advice. The idea of a priestly companion in all aspects of life exists everywhere in Orthodoxy and in Russia still today. The Startsy of the nineteenth century frequently had to take into account the resistance of the hierarchy or of the local clergy, because they took up functions that could not be placed into the customary ecclesiastical structures. Today, too, one can hear occasionally the criticism of church leaders about an exaggerated Startsism. This is partly because in the Soviet period relations between the Startsy and those they advised could only develop in a very informal and private realm. After the end of repressions, many individuals obviously also acted as Starets without the necessary spiritual charisma and exercised a strong influence, above all, on neophytes, that is, recent adherents of Orthodoxy.

When Startsism began to develop in the eighteenth century, there was a noteworthy monk from the Moldavian territory (today Romania or Moldavia) who was educated in Kiev, Paisiy (Velichkovskiy, 1722-94). He became a monk on Mount Athos, and then returned to his homeland. There, he became abbot of two influential monasteries; his students spread his teachings everywhere in Russia. Paisiy himself was adviser to many visitors. He introduced cenobite monasticism according to the Athos model. But it always was in a certain tension with the individual style of life of the ascetics and with the way of life of the Startsy who concentrated on advice and spiritual guidance for the lives of other monks. For Paisiy, the communal life in the monastery was of great significance;

later on, Startsy combined, in part, both aspects, but with a tendency toward the life of a hermit.

Paisiy's translation of the *Philokalia* is of great significance for the development of spirituality in Russia. It is one of the collection of patristic writings on spirituality, originating at Athos, that includes, above all, the Jesus Prayer, or Prayer of the Heart. This prayer consists of a brief formula, like "Lord Jesus, have mercy on me!" or, expanded, "Lord Jesus, Son of the Living God, have mercy on me, poor sinner!" This sentence is repeated again and again, often in accord with one's own breathing. It is meant to enable the worshiper to catch vision of God. This practice is to be understood in the context of theological disputes at Athos in the fourteenth century. The Jesus Prayer had, and still has, great importance for Russian spirituality. The *Philokalia* had been disseminated in manuscript for a long time at Athos, but was not printed before 1782. Paisiy translated it into Church Slavonic and thus made it available to Russian monks. A Russian edition of 1877 had an enormous effect in Russia. The Jesus Prayer became the plumb line of spiritual life for ascetics living in solitude and also in the monasteries. There, however, it had to prevail as the practice of individual, personal piety against the emphasis of the communal prayer of the church, which many monks considered traditionally to be sufficient. Although the "Spiritual Prayer" from Athos had been known earlier in Russia, the Jesus Prayer occasioned a new accentuation and a revival that, first of all, affected only monks but later affected also the spirituality of the laity.

From the Moldavian territory, Paisiy, through his writings, as well as through migrating monks, affected much of Russia. His monasteries became popular goals of pilgrimages, especially on the way from Russia to Mount Athos. So he became the most important pioneer for the further development of Russian monasticism.

Tikhon of Zadonsk (1724-83), another Starets, was bishop of Voronezh from 1763 until 1767; there he strove to enhance the educational level of his clergy; after his retirement, he became a simple monk in the monastery Zadonsk. He can be considered a forerunner of the Startsy of the nineteenth century to the extent that he was an adviser and spiritual companion of people far beyond the monastery. His contributions to spiritual literature are well known. They were influenced by German Protestant mysticism, and they also focus on the idea of the imitation of Christ as a spiritual principle. The Russian Church canonized him in 1861.

One of the most renowned Starets, in general, was Serafim of Sarov (1759-1833). In 1779 he entered the Sarov monastery as a young man and attracted attention through strict ascetic exercise, as well as through several visions that were bestowed on him. After a few years he moved to a hermitage near the monastery, where he spent his monastic life in ascetic solitude. From 1804 until 1807, he lived as a stylite on a platform, and from 1807 until 1815 he lived in total silence; after 1810, he no longer left his cell. After 1825, he began to be effective as a Starets by reaching thousands of people. He received numerous visitors and kept up an extended correspondence. The Russian Church canonized him in 1903.

Bishop Ignatius (Bryanchaninov, d. 1867) was another example of a Starets who had been a member of the hierarchy and was highly educated. After some time as a military officer, he became a monk and finally bishop in the Caucasus. After a few years, he relinquished his office and withdrew to a monastery. He authored numerous ascetic writings, as well as works for the instruction of monks. He also was effective through a busy correspondence.

The highly educated monk Feofan (Govorov), the Recluse (d. 1894), who for years lived in total solitude, enjoys high esteem still today. Already as a monk in Kiev, Novgorod, and St. Petersburg, he was active as an academic teacher and stayed in Jerusalem as well as in Constantinople. In 1859, he became a bishop, but withdrew to a hermitage after seven years where he spent his remaining twenty-eight years mostly in complete solitude. He did not receive any visitors and was connected with many people through correspondence. In the years of his confinement, he wrote numerous ascetic and exegetical works, and he translated writings about prayer and spiritual life into Russian, among them the *Philokalia*.

In conclusion, just an elucidating observation: it is the nature of church-historical sources to concentrate on official documents and actions of church administrations. In these sources, such men are named who were important for the development of the church. Women hardly ever are named. But from the beginning, there was feminine monastic life in Russia. Nuns played a significant role in Russian church history because their monasteries were devoted much more to charitable activity than the ones occupied by men. Nunneries were places of retreat for unmarried or widowed members of the nobility (also for those who were to be done away with for dynastic reasons), with whom much work was done. In the time of the Soviet Union, there were always more monasteries for women than for men, and still today, there are about twice as many nuns as monks. Nuns of the Russian emigration revived the monastic life in Serbia after World War I, after there was virtually no longer a monasticism. Women are still today blocked from advancing to higher ecclesiastical positions. But the course of Russian church history would have been different without the activity of nuns.

CHAPTER EIGHT

Spirituality and Religiosity

S pirituality is often seen as a special feature of Russian Orthodoxy. There are even stereotypes about a Russian soul that is especially "endowed," indeed, even about the size of the country and its climatic conditions. In fact, spirituality, piety, is a phenomenon of various characteristics, found in all Christian churches. Some specific features of Orthodoxy do not only apply to the Russian Church, just as some features apply only to Russian Orthodoxy. Here, no survey of the history of piety in Russia can be offered. Only two aspects are to be elucidated as examples: (1) the "Prayer of the Heart" and icon piety, and (2) the present situation of religiosity, as far as it can be comprehended and presented on the basis of sociological studies.

Basically, spirituality in Orthodoxy is always strongly marked by the church. The liturgy as the prayer of the church has great significance. Phenomena, such as a eucharistic piety independent of the liturgical celebration, were never developed in Orthodoxy. For icons, which are very important for Orthodox piety, there are relatively strict ecclesiastical prescriptions relating to their production and consecration. Prayer books with ecclesiastical prayers play a large role, as do the strict regulations of the church for fasting, which are observed by many believers. Thus, a large part of Orthodox piety is liturgically marked. An additional characteristic is its Christocentric mysticism. There are, to be sure, a pronounced veneration of saints and a Marian piety. But the liturgical prayer texts, for example, show that the saints are invoked always in relation to Christ. Orthodoxy never developed an autonomous Marian mysticism as was the case in the West.

The "Prayer of the Heart"

In addition to liturgical piety, the monastic influence is also important. From Mount Athos, one of the most important writings on spirituality spread in the Orthodox world and so also in Russia — the *Philokalia*. The title means "love for the beautiful," frequently rendered as "love for virtue." Indeed, nothing aesthetically beautiful is meant, but what is ethically good.

The *Philokalia* is a collection of texts from the church fathers throughout many centuries, containing, above all, the Jesus Prayer, also called "Prayer of the Heart" or "Perpetual Prayer." This practice of praying is to be seen in connection with the Hesychast dispute at Athos in the fourteenth century. Monks who had a mystical experience through the use of the prayer and interpreted it as a vision of God and as a vision of the transfigured Christ,[1] came into conflict with others who disputed this because God could not be viewed. The dispute was finally settled by Gregorios Palamas (d. 1359), who, through the development of a doctrine of divine energies, created the foundations for a theological doctrine that gained new significance in Orthodoxy in the twentieth century.

The prayer technique of the monks consisted in the repetition of a brief sentence, saying, "Lord Jesus Christ, have mercy on me!" This formula could also be varied, in the first part to "Lord Jesus Christ, Son of the Living God," or, in the second part to "grant me, a poor sinner, mercy!" The prayer was repeated in silence and effected in the praying believers a great internal and external peace (*hesychia* in Greek), so that the designation "Hesychasm" was created, often expanded in modernity through the adjective "palamitic." The practice of prayer was also linked to speaking the first part of the sentence when inhaling, the second when exhaling.

The Jesus Prayer became known and popular through the translation of the *Philokalia*, first into Church Slavonic and later into Russian. A special testimony for its significance is the anonymous "Honest Tales of a Pilgrim for His Spiritual Father," written toward the end of the nineteenth century. It appeared in many editions and is also available in English.[2] In

---

1. See Mark 9:2-13. Tradition identifies the place of the transfiguration as Mount Tabor. That is why the vision is also described as "Tabor Light."

2. There are several English translations, e.g., *The Way of a Pilgrim, and A Pilgrim Continues His Way*, trans. Olga Savin (Boston: Shambhala, 2001).

it, an itinerant narrator, who is on his way through Russia, records his experiences with the prayer. The *Philokalia,* which he carries with him together with the Bible, is the most important guide for his spiritual life. He reports how a Starets slowly instructed him in the exercise of the prayer and how he increased, according to the instruction, the number of the prayers to 12,000 per day. After a time, it became a habit so that he could be at it while engaging in all other activities. Finally, the pilgrim writes about the experience that the prayer performed by itself: "it prays in me." This experience of praying is connected with other experiences, for example, with great warmth permeating the body. This also corresponds to the descriptions of the Fathers, contained in the *Philokalia,* which the pilgrim understands better and better with progressive prayer practice. Warmth and light are the most frequent manifestations reported. Such experiences are transmitted by many mystics, not only from the Christian domain. The designation "perpetual prayer" can be traced, on the one hand, to 1 Thessalonians 5:17 ("pray without ceasing") and, on the other hand, to the phenomenon that it is performed "by itself," that is, not through an active decision of the one who prays. Orthodox monks and nuns, but also many laypeople, carry a prayer chain around the wrist, or in the hand, mostly knotted by wool; with its help the Jesus Prayer exercise can be performed. But this prayer practice is not like the one with the Western rosary where a certain sequence must be spoken that must be counted down with the chain. Rather, the Jesus Prayer is an exercise of piety that is performed daily in the monastery or in the world and transmits a special spiritual experience to the one who prays.

The tales of the "pilgrim" take up an additional motive that is important for Russian spirituality, namely, that of wandering or roaming about. Originally, the "wanderers" *(stranniki)* were one of the sects among Old Believers who had no priests, and were marked by being homeless and by roaming around, thus evading public control. So it was understood as a special form of asceticism. Many traveled through the country and often went on long journeys to famous monasteries or places of pilgrimage, also to Palestine, or to Mount Athos. The "Honest Tales" made this phenomenon famous. Such wanderers frequently encountered the distrust of the authorities because controlling them was simply not possible.

Another special form of asceticism was letting oneself be ridiculed. The so-called "fools for Christ's sake" *(yurodivyye* in Russian) were people who, for religious reasons, pretended to be dumb, allowed themselves to be laughed at, to be illogical, and be out of sync with social traditions.

They achieved the same effect by abandoning hygiene, or any normal civil behavior. Already the chronicle of the Kiev Cave Monastery knows a monk named Isaac who lived as a "fool in Christ." The fools for Christ's sake call to mind the practices of ascetics in ancient church history. Dostoyevskiy memorialized this phenomenon in the figure of Prince Myshkin in his novel *The Idiot*.

All these outward manifestations show that the detractions, to which Russian Orthodoxy was exposed as an established church, were not able to suppress its spiritual dynamics but only provided new forms of expression. The common theological background of all these forms of asceticism is the effort to ascertain whatever can be understood as encounters with God and thus attain salvation. Mysticism discovered various forms of expression: sight (or visual perception) of God, indwelling, experience of God, encounter with God, and many others. For the Orthodox tradition, the theological notion is important that salvation is understood as *theosis*, a Greek idea that can only inadequately be translated as "deification" or "divinization." It expresses that it is possible for a human being to become like God — "participants of the divine nature" (2 Pet. 1:4). Behind it is the notion that through the incarnation of the Son of God — that is, God becoming human — the reverse process is possible. Just as God accepted human nature, so human nature can be united with God. This is expressed with the term *theosis*. According to this understanding, the goal of all human endeavor is to become God, and the ascetics try to attain this goal through their efforts.

The Jesus Prayer is primarily a monastic prayer practice. The texts are from monks and are meant to be for monks. It is characteristic for Orthodox, and perhaps also for the special Russian spirituality, that it knows no other rules than the ones for the laity. The piety of the Orthodox Christian in the world is basically not different from that of an inhabitant of a monastery. This is evident by the fact that in most parishes the Hours, at least the Vespers, are a public (and normally well-attended) worship service, by the duration of the services, as well as by the strict rules of fasting, the observation of which is also demanded from the laity.

Iconic Piety

Orthodox images of veneration, icons are an especially important part of spirituality in the church as well as in the piety of the working day in the

Christian East. This becomes quite evident during visits in an Orthodox household or while sightseeing in an Orthodox Church.

The Russian Church accepted Byzantine Christianity after the conclusion of the iconoclast controversy (about 730-843), that is, with an elaborated theology of icons. In the meantime, icons had become, as it were, the distinguishing mark of Orthodoxy. Icons were placed on the barriers of demarcation between the chancel and the nave that had existed since the ancient church, so that a wall of icons developed, the iconostasis, that separated the altar space from the space for the believers, or, according to the understanding of many Orthodox theologians, connected them with each other. Whoever visits an Orthodox church for the first time will first notice that the altar cannot be seen because a high wall displaying icons is placed in front of it. After the victory of the icons, the iconostases became higher and higher; some of them go up to the ceiling of the church. Frequently, they are no longer simply wooden walls but edifices built within edifices, some built with marble. In addition, the church walls are painted with frescoes. Only most recently, sporadic efforts have been undertaken to build low iconostases that grant believers a view of the altar.

In every church, icons are lying on lecterns ready to be venerated. These are not just any icons but, as a rule, icons for holy days (or feast days), celebrated on the preceding Sunday, and for the patron of the church. There is also a set program for the arrangement of images on the iconostasis. The program can vary, to be sure, and can be expanded, but it is not to be changed in its foundations. Orthodox believers who enter a church venerate first the main icons in the center of the nave. The veneration occurs through making the sign of the cross, bowing or prostrating before the image, and kissing the icons. Often also candles are lit before the icons; the candles can be bought at the entrance of the church. The veneration of the images happens during the worship service as well as outside of it. Disgraceful behavior before icons meets with displeasure: in strict parishes, if one turns one's back, keeps one's hands in the back, or, as a woman, wears trousers.

Icons also play a significant role for piety in the personal, individual domain. Every residence contains a "beautiful corner" where some icons hang, usually behind small, burning oil lamps. Orthodox Christians who enter the room bow and make the sign of the cross before these icons. This is where one usually prays. Moreover, one should not display improper behavior before them in the residence. There is a tradition of turning the icons around if one quarrels. Children receive small icons at baptism (or are endowed with icons, at times in the length of the new-born baby). An icon is given to the deceased in the coffin. There are small icons for travelers, transportable and protected for the journey so that they can be placed at another location.

What is the theological conception behind this relation to icons? The idea of "cult images" indicates that a cult, a veneration, is connected with them. In the theology of images that originated in connection with the iconoclast controversy, the conception prevailed that the image partici-pates in its archetype, that in the presentation of a person there also is al-ways something of this person present. We know this from our secular domain of experience, when we carry with us pictures of people impor-tant to us, or have them in range of sight. Such images are not only un-derstood as recollections, but make the depicted person present; this presence is sometimes felt so strongly that it is for many people a difficult idea to destroy such a picture. If the picture contains the reality of what is depicted and guarantees a kind of presence, and if Jesus Christ, depicted on the icon, is true man and true God, as the Christian creed affirms, then God is present in the icon of Christ. In this logic, it goes without saying that a special veneration is due to this picture. If, and because, the picture secures the presence of God, prayers before the icon, devout veneration, and special respect are self-evident for believers.

Accordingly, with icons the point is not a naturalistic representation. The opponents of images argued that God may not be represented — ac-cording to the prohibition of pictures in the Old Testament (Deut. 5:8) — and that therefore no pictures are thinkable. The supporters prevailed, in the end, with the argument that, even though the divine nature cannot be depicted, certainly the divine incarnation in the person of Jesus can. After all, his contemporaries saw him during his earthly life. Icons, therefore, do not show Christ as realistically as possible, but in a defined style. The possibility of an unrestrained depiction is even more confined by a tradi-tion of various miraculous icons, such as icons that fell from the sky, or the impression of Christ's face on a cloth for which a king asked. The is-sue is not, therefore, whether to make the picture reflect as much as is possible the model or archetype. Rather, the presence of what is repre-sented should be rendered possible through the picture. It is not the pur-pose of icons to show someone or something the way it looks, but to cre-ate a presence of the one who is depicted.

Painters of icons, who are often monks (or nuns), do not view their activity as art but as a religious act for which they prepare themselves through prayer and fasting. It is not their desire to bring their own accent to the formation of icons; rather, the patterns are to be reproduced as faithfully as possible. Correspondingly, the believers also do not understand icons as art but as a mysterious presence of God in the world. To outsiders, icons create the effect of having been "punched," without any artistic innovation. But that is the intention of the painters on the basis of various schools. It is, of course, also possible to identify some painters, although they set no value on an appearance through an individual style or a personal note. According to such an understanding, icons also do not belong to a museum or to a collection in Orthodox thinking. They are cultic objects and, as such, are to be available for veneration. According to Orthodox understanding, the question is completely irrelevant whether a picture is a "true" icon, that is, the question about the age, the painter, or the material value. In the final analysis, an icon is a stick-on transfer of an image to plywood, just like an old picture painted by hand. To understand icons and iconic theology, one must abandon the idea that it is a question of artistic production. That may be the case from a perspective of art history. But it is not significant for a theological understanding of icons.

Theological concepts were developed for the veneration of icons. Russian theology adopted, for the time being, the theology of icons that had merged in the eighth and ninth centuries in connection with the iconoclastic controversy. John of Damascus, Germanos of Constantinople, and Theodor Studites are the most important names of that time. At that time, the controversies dealt with christological questions, that is, who Jesus Christ is and how divinity and humanity relate to each other. After that, there was no important further development of the theology of images, and there also was no need for Russian authors to produce works for the defense of images. But in the twentieth century, Pavel Florenskiy did publish two writings (*The Iconostasis* and *The Reverse Perspective*, with a sharp criticism of the Western religious painting). There is also a book by Sergiy Bulgakov titled *Icons and the Veneration of Icons*. A series of authors in the exile dealt with the Eastern theology of images, perhaps stimulated through the encounter with the Christian West and its totally different ideas of pictures.

The present practice of the veneration of icons frequently goes beyond what the classical Greek authors advocated. To counter the accusation of venerating idols, it was always important to them to make the issue not the picture as such, that is, wood and colors, but the presence of the depicted person. An icon on which the person cannot be recognized could, therefore, be viewed like any piece of wood. But today, icons that can no longer be used because of the soot generated by the candles placed before them are treated with greatest reverence; they are either buried or burned. The idea of the presence of who is depicted, according to the ancient authors, also always knows of the unlikeness between the archetype and the copy; thus it does not allow any confusion of the two. Popular religious ideas go far beyond that, such as the notion that the icon "sees" what is happening in a room, or that icons are "windows into eternity." Only authors of the twentieth century developed the theology of icons further and tried to defend such notions.

Iconic piety tries to meet the need of people to materialize their religious ideas, that is, to have something that is tangible, visible, and thus available in a certain sense. This corresponds to a basic anthropological component against which also Christianity was not extensively immune, because of its adoption of the Jewish legacy. Christianity existed without images for centuries. The christological considerations of what can be depicted concerned only pictures of Jesus; there are (and were) also icons of Mary, of other saints, even of events, and icons serving as calendars (through images of the respective saints for each day). Iconic theological principles applied only a little, if at all, to such icons. Nevertheless, today they are offered the same veneration as the icons of Christ — a sign not only of how far the practice of icons has developed beyond theoretical principles, but also of the attempt to satisfy the aforementioned basic need to materialize religion.

Although painting icons is not meant to be art, icons can be considered from the point of view of art history. If so, then a development of various schools can be recognized in Russia, distinguished by stylistic peculiarities. First, Greek, then Western influences can be detected. The icon painter Feofan Grek ("the Greek") may serve as an example. He worked in the 1370s in Russia and painted the Kremlin cathedrals at the turn to the fifteenth century. He and his contemporary, Andrey Rublev, represent a culmination of Russian icon painting. In the course of the fifteenth century, the influence of Bulgarians, Serbs, and Greeks increased because of the Ottoman expansion and immigration from these regions to Russia. In the Western territories, the later Latin influence is unmistakable, so that icons originate marked by baroque painting in formation and motivation.

Icons that represent persons were basically produced only of Christ and of saints. In the 1990s, one could see in Russia more and more icons that represented the last tsar, Nikolay II. For a long time the church resisted the idea of canonizing the tsar. When the mortal remains of the tsar family were taken from the place of their execution, Yekaterinburg (Sverdlovsk in the Soviet time), to the burial place of the Romanovs in St. Petersburg, President Yeltsin participated, but no representative of the church did. The leadership of the church was under increasing pressure, incited by interested circles, but also by a steadily growing veneration, manifested in icons. Finally, in the summer of 2000 the tsar and his family were canonized (together with hundreds of other martyrs of the Soviet regime). Icons that originated before this act were interpreted as signs of Sobornost, that is, the notion that the truth was to be found in the people of God already prior to an official ecclesiastical decision.

Religious Practice Today

The present landscape of religions and religiosity in Russia is very colorful. Besides people who belong to the ROC, or to one of the smaller religious communities, there are many who call themselves simply "Christians," and of course, there are nonreligious people, mostly agnostics, but also atheists. However, the boundaries between these groups are blurred. Precisely, representatives of the Communist Party frequently form coalitions with politicians who understand themselves to be Orthodox, and use the terminology of Orthodoxy to gain sympathy and votes. In 1999 a book appeared in Moscow with the title *Faith and Loyalty (Vera i vernost')* and the subtitle *Problems of the Religious Rebirth of Russia;* on the inside of the cover one could see an icon of the Blessed Virgin, and in the book there was the portrait of the author in front of a church flag. He was no less than Gennadiy Zyuganov, the chairman of the Russian Communist Party. Numerous examples could be cited furnishing evidence that the present religious situation in Russia is a colorful field.

In the years since the end of the Soviet Union, it has been possible to conduct, without any great restrictions, sociological surveys on religion. Previously there were only a few such surveys, which were conducted for purposes of information for the Communist Party with great secrecy. There are no longer any administrative restrictions. But another problem surfaces, namely, the lack of adequate methodology. With the exception of the former Yugoslavia, there was hardly any religious-sociological research in the Communist countries, and researchers were, and still are, strongly influenced by Western methods. But it is not clear what kinds of questions must be asked to comprehend Orthodox religiosity. Typically "Catholic" questions, such as those regarding attendance at the Sunday liturgy, or typically "Protestant" ones, such as those about the possession or reading of the Bible, can secure interesting insights. But they do not establish a picture of the actual religiosity in Russia.

The attempt to assess the religious practice today is complicated by the fact that the numerous surveys of recent years reveal a totally unstable situation. The number of people who call themselves Orthodox has changed very much. Questions like "Are you Orthodox?" or "Do you belong to the Orthodox Church?" yielded strongly different results: Orthodoxy as a sign of identity was not necessarily linked to a concrete organization. In 2002, a census was conducted in which questions about belonging to religion were not asked. There were rumors that this was done on request of the ROC, which did not trust the authorities and was afraid that the number of members would be much fewer than its own evidence showed and, above all, might indicate its own public importance.

On a representative survey of 1,600 Russian inhabitants in more than 100 locations, conducted in the summer of 2005, the question was asked, "Irrespective of whether or not you attend a worship service, would you say you are . . . ?" From the three listed possibilities, 57 percent chose the answer "a religious person," 36 percent responded "not a religious person," and 4 percent said "a convinced atheist." The remaining 3 percent responded with "I do not know," or did not provide an answer.

The analysis of the answers reveals that such a question would yield the same responses in other countries. Women declare themselves religious more frequently than do men; less educated and poorer people more frequently claim to be religious than those on a higher educational level; and pensioners more than any other part of the population classify themselves as religious. The highest number of those who declared themselves not to be religious were residents of large cities with more than 500,000 inhabitants. But there is a significant difference in western European societies. The number of young people between eighteen and twenty-four who were not religious was just above average, 58 percent; the next age group (twenty-four to thirty-five) was the lowest, 49 percent.

According to the same survey, the percentage of Russians attending church is as low as anywhere in Europe. The number that said they attended church every week begins in the various surveys with 2 percent, then moves higher, but never up to a two-figure number.[3] Although one can also observe similar divergences in western European countries, especially in countries with churches established by the state (Scandinavia), or with church taxes, the question is still to be asked what it means to call oneself a religious person in a "Christian" country without relating it to church attendance.

It is interesting that among people who declared themselves "Orthodox," 97 percent said they believed in God — therefore, no more than 3 percent of the "Orthodox" do not believe in God. Among Russians who declare themselves not to be religious, 29.6 percent believe in God. Of those who declared themselves to be Orthodox, 27.9 percent pray every day (outside the worship service), and 5.4 percent attend church every week and 11 percent every month, according to their own testimony. The fact that the number of those who pray regularly is much higher than the number of those who attend church indicates that there is an "Orthodoxy beyond the walls of the church,"[4] that is, a form of Orthodox religiosity that cannot be determined by the numbers of those who attend church.

The different categories of "religiosity" and "church membership" have been introduced to better understand the conditions in Russia. Both can only be described through a combination of indicators. To clarify church membership, questions are used, such as faith in God, regular church attendance and receiving Holy Communion with confession, observation of rules for fasting, and the use of ecclesiastical prayer books at home. The result indicates that only a small number of those who describe themselves as "Orthodox Christians" can be called completely enchurched; most of those who responded were only to the least extent enchurched. Assisted by such investigations, various scholars concluded that the portion of the Orthodox "church incorporated" is no greater than 5-7 percent of the population. They are often called "real," "traditional," or "ecclesiastical" Orthodox; the rest are "nominal" or "cultural Orthodox."

Such results of surveys point to several phenomena: within the group of those who call themselves "religious" or "Orthodox," there are obvi-

---

3. Detlef Pollack, "Religiöser Wandel in Mittel und Osteuropa," in *Religiöser Wandel in den postkommunistischen Ländern Ost-und Mitteleuropas,* ed. Detlef Pollack et al. (Würzburg: Ergon, 1998), 9-52. Or Kimmo Kääriänen, *Religion in Russia after the Collapse of Communism* (Lewiston, N.Y.: Edwin Mellen Press, 1998), especially 112.

4. The title of the dissertation of Inna Naletova (Boston University, 2007).

ously considerable differences. The self-designation alone is not at all sufficient to describe the religiosity of the Russian people. Besides, the largest part of Orthodox believers in Russia today is "neophytes," that is, people who came to Orthodoxy only in recent years. They frequently distinguish themselves through a special radicalism that is accompanied by exceedingly little knowledge of Christian and Orthodox principles, and, quite often, they take over the role of "guardians" of the purity of Orthodoxy. Diffuse ideas and rigorous attitudes about many questions of religious life are the result.

Furthermore, it becomes evident that religiosity does not have to play an important role in daily life. Among the "religious," only about 60 percent declared that God plays an important role in their lives. Thus there need not be a correspondence between religious faith and daily life; one can be religious without any consequences for one's actions.

On the other hand, in the surveys, the church is an institution that enjoys great trust, more, in any case, than political or public institutions. Accordingly, the church is frequently understood as an institution whose existence is considered important even if one is not religious oneself. Many people declare religion and faith in God not important for themselves, but they are convinced that the Orthodox Church is a trustworthy institution and that its existence is important for Russia.

Many parareligious manifestations can be observed in Russia today. Faith in astrology, in UFOs, and in numerous other supernatural phenomena is widespread, even among people who call themselves Orthodox. Again and again, there are reports about miraculous healers, and again and again, groups and movements arise, led by charismatic personalities and having recourse to Orthodox terminology or symbolism. For many people, faith in such things obviously does not contradict their Orthodox religiosity.

It becomes evident that "Orthodoxy" in Russia today not only describes the Orthodox Church but is also code for many other things. The phenomenon that people who call themselves Orthodox do not believe in God, or do not present themselves somehow as Orthodox in their lives, indicates that the category "Orthodox" is used for forming an identity. This is clearly so since the end of the Soviet Union, which, of course, also meant an end of a given and generally accepted system of values and norms. Many people obviously filled the resulting vacuum with the affirmation of something handed down, namely, Orthodoxy, without having always been conscious of the contents and consequences of such an affirmation.

Orthodoxy and Identity

The important role of Orthodoxy as an identity marker can be shown in numerous domains relating to religiosity as well as to the relation between church and state, or between Russian Orthodoxy and the West. There are also similar phenomena in Western churches and societies. But in all these cases religion has another function than the one it ascribes to itself. A religious association will never understand itself as a means to achieve a national, political, or any other identity. Religions are convictions that want to explain the world and the human being, and offer a way to liberate humanity from an unsalvageable situation. This leads also to a formation of identities, but it is not the primary purpose of religion according to its own understanding.

Historically, above all, Christian denominations have very strongly contributed to the formation of national identities. That is especially true for eastern Europe. The difference between Protestant Prussians, Roman Catholic Poles, and the Greek-Catholic Ukrainians (as well as the Jews) was decisive in nineteenth-century Galicia. There the religious differentiation has contributed to the establishment of a Ukrainian national self-consciousness just as it has with Catholic Croats, Orthodox Serbians, and Muslim Bosniacs. The Orthodox Church became especially important for the development of nations because of its organizational structure and because it developed a close relationship with the nations during the enduring Ottoman rule in all Orthodox territories except Russia.

In his disputed book *The Clash of Civilizations,* the American political scientist Samuel Huntington describes the line between Orthodoxy and Western denominations as the most important demarcation in Europe.[5] Even if one rejects the vision of Europe which informs the worldview of Huntington, one must indeed ask why the Eastern nations, marked by Orthodoxy, obviously have greater difficulties with democratization after 1989 than the nations originating from a Catholic or Protestant tradition. One can cite the authoritarian past that not only does not know any democratic traditions but in which also the development of a society began very late. It was customary to speak of tsarist Russia as "society arranged by the state." The great difficulties in the origin of civil societies in these countries can be traced to this historical burden.

5. Samuel P. Huntington, *The Clash of Civilizations and the Remaking of World Order* (New York: Simon and Schuster, 1996).

At the same time, the ROC speaks very critically not only of the Western ideas of civil society and democracy, but also of other values that belong to the core of society in the West, especially human rights. Some top-ranking representatives of the church pointed out that this is because Western concepts have no validity for Orthodoxy and for Russia. In the summer of 2005, the director of the Department for External Church Relations, Metropolitan Kirill (Gundyayev), the present patriarch, called "unity and agreement" the foundations of Russian democracy[6] — a modern interpretation of Sobornost, but also a demarcation from Western concepts for which, of course, pluralism and competition of ideas are constitutive.

Russian Orthodoxy basically advocated for many centuries the ideas of the state that also marked the respective Russian state. This implies that Orthodoxy completely joined the imperial development of Russia and thus was the church of the Orthodox in the Russian Empire; this can be clearly demonstrated especially among Ukrainians and Georgians. Also the "pagans," adherents of traditional religions, were converted to Orthodoxy when Russia conquered the respective territories and people; frequently, executive power was used. A mission to the Muslims was also attempted, albeit without success. Russian Orthodoxy viewed itself as superior to these religions, and it could exist with the conviction to be, if not the majority, then the elite in the Russian Empire. The emergence of national ideas in the nineteenth century disclosed also nationalistic activities of Russian Orthodoxy, for example, in regard to Ukraine and its ecclesiastical efforts. But basically, the Russian Church represented an imperial attitude due to its position in the empire. This attitude also explains its relative toleration of other religions. On the other hand, the smaller Orthodox churches in southeastern Europe could not form any imperial consciousness because of historical circumstances. But they could concentrate on their own nation and consider Muslims "properly" as members of their own nation. Such national tendencies in Russian Orthodoxy become completely clear only in the present, conditioned by the fact that millions of Orthodox Russians lived, for the first time, outside of Russia. The Russians are a "delayed nation" insofar as the state "created" a nation. The church — being first more strongly connected with the state, and now also with the nation — now supported, for example, the

---

6. See www.kirchen-in-osteuropa.de/archiv/05080402.htm#19/. Nachrichten-dienst Östliche Kirchen, Teil B, August 4, 2005.

interests of Russian pensioners in Latvia whose pensions are not paid. It is now concerned with Russians abroad, motivated by an unambiguous national position.

The offer of identity, which Orthodoxy today represents in Russia, is closely tied with the Russian nation, but also with the historical greatness of Russia (and not infrequently of the Soviet Union). It, therefore, is closely linked to being Russian and easily connects with other national ideas. This can lead to peculiar political coalitions that really do not correspond with political logic. But the Communist rejection of the church in the past is not that important if both the Communists and the church advocate the same goal, namely, the restoration of Russia's greatness, which was once guaranteed by the Communists. Conversely, it is also necessary for the political Left to be open for the church and its themes because thereby a significant social factor is addressed in Russia today, linked to a positive value.

At the same time, the connection between being Russian and Orthodox results in the cultivation of traditional values through the church. Up to now, the ROC has offered conventional responses to the many challenges of modernity. The attitude toward homosexuality can serve as an example. The church reacted by qualifying the phenomenon as sin with an appeal to repent. So far, a more differentiated understanding of homosexuals, or pastoral approaches, has not appeared. Modern Russia is a nation where one can find the same manifestations and inquiries that exist in Western societies, even though, at times, they are delayed in arriving. In the long run, the church will isolate itself with such positions from the trends of modernity and lose much of its social significance.

CHAPTER NINE

Russian Orthodoxy and the West

R ussian church history can be read as the attempt of the church to
find strategies against Western influences that were perceived as a
threat. This has to do with the efforts of the Catholic Church to gain influence on the territory of the Rus', especially after Lithuania decided in
favor of the Catholic Church. Likewise, this has to do with the unions in
which Orthodox dioceses, belonging to Moscow, were asked to accept
another ecclesiastical affiliation; one such union failed at Florence, another was successful at Brest. Furthermore, the rejection of the ecclesiastical structure of Peter I is related to theological influences and models
that found their way to Russia via Kiev, and later directly. The rejection
goes as far as the modern phenomena, labeled "Western" and mostly
qualified with catchwords like "liberalism" and "individualism," that were
to summarize, above all, ideas of the Enlightenment. It may be viewed as
an irony of history that Western influences still crept in and marked Russian Orthodoxy. Even the great enemies of the West rely on a Western
concept with their emphasis on the nation.

Influence and Threat

The constant argument with the West is linked to the geographical location of Russia. In the north, the polar sea constituted the boundary of the
settled space; in the east, there was the wideness of Siberia, in particular,
the steppe; in the south, the Caucasus and the Black Sea were the border
to the Islamic world; in the southwest, there was Ukraine with its chang-

ing history of dominion and the Carpathian Mountains as the natural border to the Balkans. But in the west, there was the always changing borders to the Western countries of Poland and Lithuania. The transfer of the Rus', from Kiev to the north, that is, the northeast, initiated first an isolation of the empire from the rest of Europe. At the time of the altercation with the Tartars, the stance toward the West was defensive against campaigns of the Swedes and of the Teutonic Order. These events have become deeply imprinted in the collective memory, or, more precisely, they could be reproduced from there again and again.

A gradual turn to the West was connected with the final stabilization of Moscow and the independence of the Orthodox Church, as well as with the political changes of the sixteenth century. The Moscow empire enjoyed a growing attention because it had become a factor in international relations that could no longer be ignored. Even though there were no dynastic relations with western European reigning families between the twelfth and sixteenth centuries,[1] Russia was now considered a partner in the concert of European countries, despite its bordering position and lack of information about "Moscowia." The number of Western embassies increased. Besides the growing number of Greeks, who came to Moscow after the end of the Byzantine Empire, there were, above all, Italians who assisted in the fashioning of the Kremlin. The first reports about Russia reached the West through such contacts. Most widely read was the one of the Hapsburg ambassador Herberstein, who was in Russia in 1516-17 and 1526-27. Considerably later, in 1549, he published *Peculiar Moscovite Stories (Rerum Moscoviticarum Commentarii)*. With this book, which assessed Russia according to Western standards and presented it very negatively, he marked the German and European image of Russia for a long time, since there were English reports of travelers visiting Russia only some time later. Since Herberstein also had been instructed to examine the statements of a Russian embassy, his writing contains a series of observations about church affairs. This flow of information went almost exclusively in one direction, since there were no Russian travel reports about the West and very few Russian travelers to western Europe. Only the reforms of Peter provided any opportunity to learn to know the West better; and only through Russian soldiers who reached

---

1. See Hans-Joachim J. Torke, *Einführung in die Geschichte Russlands* (Munich: C. H. Beck, 1997), 35. Torke even writes that the "dynastic marriages . . . were thwarted by the Orthodox side."

Paris in the wars against Napoleon, did a greater extent of news from and about the West reach Russia.

Already at the turn from the fifteenth to the sixteenth century, there was a period of Italian influence in Moscow. Under Ivan III and his Byzantine wife Zoe (or, respectively, "Sophia"), Italian master builders were brought to change and expand the Moscow Kremlin. This influence is clearly evident in the two most important and largest churches in the Kremlin, the Dormition Cathedral and the Cathedral of the Archangels, where the tombs of the Moscow princes, and of the tsars, are situated.

With respect to church and theology, the influence was restricted almost exclusively to Kiev. Ukraine, with its location and old affiliation with the Rus', as well as through its later conquest by Lithuania and Poland, was predestined to become a connecting link between Russia and the West. Polish authorities had no interest in having Orthodox subjects under the authority of the church in Moscow. That is why they advocated the idea of union with Rome as well as conversions. The "Uniate" (but also the Orthodox) hierarchs in Poland-Lithuania strove for the education of their theologians; adherents of the union were educated in Jesuit colleges that had been established everywhere in Ukraine to provide an education for theologians from Lithuania-Poland who favored the union. The perception of Catholicism as a threat strengthened. Some of these theologians were also sent to Rome. It became clear that many of them converted back to the Orthodox Church after concluding their studies, but it cannot be determined whether calculations or a double change of convictions caused their return. In any case, the Jesuit Catholic education offered the only possibility to gain solid philosophical and theological knowledge that was not available in Russia itself. The greatest influence was not in the adoption of ideas or concepts but in the formation of Russian theology that was to maintain for centuries a Western, indeed far-reaching, scholastic form. The consequences of this influence, called the "Latin captivity" by Georges Florovsky,[2] can still be felt today, although there is a consciousness since the twentieth century that one is to return to the patristic sources.

A pronounced Protestant influence came to Russia with the reforms of Peter. The European countries that impressed Peter — England, the

2. Georges Florovsky, "Westliche Einflüsse in der russischen Theologie," in *Proces-Verbaux du premier congres de Theologie orthodoxe a Athenes,* ed. Hamlikar S. Alivisatos (Athens: Pyrsos, 1939), 212-31, at 224.

Netherlands, Prussia — were Protestant. When a calendar was introduced, Peter decided in favor of the Julian one that was used in Protestant countries; at that time, they still rejected the (more precise) Gregorian one because it came from the pope. Russia did not join the countries of Europe in adopting the Gregorian calendar, so until the Revolution of 1917 the Russian chronology was thirteen days behind the western European one. The church still uses the Julian calendar today, which is why in Russia Christmas and all other permanent holidays are celebrated thirteen days after the Western date; Easter and the days of the Easter cycle could coincide or diverge by one, four, or five weeks. There were Protestant tendencies also again and again among Peter's successors. But they did not last.

Western influences represented again and again an enticement, but were also seen as a danger that threatened the essence of Russia. The latter is to be viewed in connection with the military aggressions that came from the West, from those of the Teutonic Order to the German army in World War II. Accordingly, an important part of the perception of the West is the will to conquer; another is Western Christianity, seen as Catholic. The nearest neighbor in the West was, of course, Poland, a Catholic country, while the encounters with Protestantism were rather sporadic and less emotionally charged.

The way the West is viewed is well exemplified in a detail of recent years. Until the first years of President Putin's rule, the Day of the October Revolution was a Russian national holiday celebrated on November 7 (because of the difference in calendars!); after the end of the Soviet Union it was called the Day of Friendship and Reconciliation. In 2005, a new national holiday was established, the Day of National Unity. It is celebrated on November 4 (according to the old calendar, on October 17). On that day in 1612, at the "Time of Troubles," Russian troops reconquered the Moscow Kremlin from the Poles. The decision to establish a new holiday was not only a pragmatic act. A new commemoration day was needed at the end of Communism. It is an interpretation of history by the present Russian state that stresses unity against aggressors from the West.

The consequence of this kind of vision is the introduction of a compulsory subject in the schools, "Foundations of Orthodox Culture," which is taught in many regions. It does not deal with religious instruction but offers an introduction to Russian history and Russian thought, characterized as Orthodox history and Orthodox thought. Thus, Russia defines itself as marked by Orthodoxy, and the church does not oppose such a definition. Existing textbooks and experiences show that the beginning of instruction is not oriented by culture but is strongly oriented toward the Orthodox Church. The content of instruction stresses the special Russian path and the distance from Western values and ideas.

These observations contrast with the positive image of the West that also exists in Russia. The streets are crowded with Western automobiles, stores deal with Western goods, and the growing middle class is attracted to the same travel destinations as are western European tourists. But there are quite a few who, though enjoying the same advantages, see in them an estrangement and a threat.

Union Decrees

Already in the thirteenth century, there was the idea of a union in the Roman Church. Accordingly, the Orthodox Church of Constantinople was to acknowledge the superior authority of the pope and, in return, would be allowed to keep all its customs. The Second Council of Lyon (1274) produced the first example of a union decree. But the historical consciousness was essentially stronger in the East. For there it was known that in the first millennium the Roman bishops never had such fullness of power over the Eastern patriarchates as they now demanded. That is why the union of Lyon, as well as also its more important successor, the union of Florence (1439), could not last long.

But from a Catholic perspective, the union of Florence created a precedent, showing what such an ecclesiastical union would look like, and there were some cases in which this way of proceeding was at least partially successful. Nevertheless, all unions that still exist today created a schism of the respective Orthodox churches. The entire church never accepted the union with Rome (the Maronites in Lebanon cannot be counted as a classical union). Some bishops always favored union while others stayed with their original Eastern church. It is quite disputed to speak of "success" regarding the unions existing today, but such unions, which have existed for centuries, the so-called Greek Catholic churches (as distinguished from the Roman Catholic Church), have today their own identity and consciousness as Eastern, but not Orthodox, and as Catholic, but not Latin, churches; and people who identify themselves with such a church are, of course, entitled to receive pastoral care.

The first encounter with the notion of union in Russia, namely, the attempt to accept the union of Florence in Moscow, led to the auto-cephaly of Russian Orthodoxy — in the Rus', there seemed to be no reports about the Second Council of Lyon. Already before the Council of Florence, there were attempts to reduce the ecclesiastical dependency on Constantinople, albeit without any consequences. Metropolitan Isidore, who had received the office of a Kiev metropolitan because he was thought to favor a union, stayed only briefly in Moscow before his departure to the council. In Florence, the pope appointed him cardinal legate for Lithuania, Livonia, and Russia. While returning to Moscow, he tried, without any great success, to propagate the union among the Orthodox in Lithuania. But he was not supported by the Catholic bishops who adhered to the countercouncil of Basel. Moreover, the idea of a Catholic archbishop for Lithuania residing in Moscow generated skepticism. The attempt to proclaim a union in the Kremlin ended with the arrest of Isidore.

But Rome continued to view the Russian space as a potential territory for union. The Reformation increased the role of the Catholic Church in European politics because it was a mediator and leader of the Catholic countries and remained so until the end of the Thirty Years' War in 1648. The Vatican was, of course, a political structure for it. In Poland-Lithuania, the willingness increased among Orthodox bishops to be subject to Rome, with all their believers, and maintain their own customs. Several reasons can be cited, such as the discrimination of the Orthodox in a strongly marked Catholic state, or the strong pressure of the Counter-Reformation. At a synod in 1595, all Orthodox bishops agreed to ask Rome to be accepted in the union. Two bishops were sent to Rome to negotiate. The result was not what was hoped for; the union articles were not formally confirmed by the pope but only issued by him. Moreover, the Orthodox in Poland-Lithuania were not incorporated as a church into the communion of the Catholic Church but only as individuals. But the pope granted the retention of the ritual and the unity with Rome.

After the return of the two dispatched bishops to their homeland, there was resistance against the intention of a union. At another synod in 1596, two bishops refused to sign the Roman document and staged a countersynod together with influential laypeople. Despite the coercive measures for the acceptance of the union, the once Orthodox Church was now divided into one part that was Greek Catholic, and another that wanted to remain with Orthodoxy and the communion with Moscow. In time, the "union" church became exposed to intense pressure to adjust and to measures to become Latinized so that its rite was strongly changed. It can still be discerned today as Eastern, but with many elements of the Latin Church, unknown in Orthodoxy.

The Orthodox Church was in a difficult position in Poland-Lithuania. The so-called Brotherhoods, above all, kept the Orthodox consciousness alive and tried to strengthen it through publications. The Kiev Cave Monastery and its school were considered the bulwark of Orthodoxy.

When the territories with a strong union, the present Ukraine and Belarus, became a large part of Russia in the eighteenth century, the union could not survive there. In some territories the bishops subjected themselves to the synod in St. Petersburg and so became again Orthodox. But most of the believers were forced to join the Roman Catholic Church, which created dioceses for this purpose. The union could only survive in parts of Belarus and especially in west-Ukrainian Galicia, which was under Hapsburg rule after the divisions in Poland and belonged to Poland between the two world wars. Especially under Tsar Alexander III (1881-94) were there new efforts to make the western territories of the empire more Russian where the union had been strong.

After World War II, the Polish borders shifted toward the west and Galicia became part of the Soviet Ukraine. The authorities called a "synod" together in 1946, and some priests and laypeople of the Greek Catholic Church subjected themselves to the Moscow patriarchy. But no bishops attended the synod, and none ever agreed with the decision. All the bishops died in prison, except the head of the church, Grand Archbishop Josef Slipiy, who was allowed to travel from a Soviet prison camp in 1963 to the Second Vatican Council and lived in Rome until his death in 1984. The Soviet rulers forced the unification with the Russian Church. Priests could choose between accepting the agreement or being arrested.

But a Greek Catholic underground church endured in the Soviet Union. There were bishops and priests, a secret monastic life, and rudimentary theological education. Church services were held in private residences or out-of-doors. An extremely careful relation could be maintained with the Ukrainian church in exile, which had its center in Rome and some dioceses in the West, above all in the USA and in Canada. Most of the priests of the ROC came from territories where the union was strong and where there were more parishes than in other parts of the country.

In connection with the *perestroika*, the first representatives of the

Greek Catholic Church dared to appear in public. At the end of 1989 it was possible for parishes to officially register with the authorities. Many priests and believers, as well as entire parishes, moved like a landslide from Russian Orthodoxy to the Greek Catholic Church. Even violence was not rare because the property of church buildings was disputed. Russian Orthodoxy lost most of its parishes in the region, especially since two other competing Orthodox churches split from it, that is, established themselves. The Russian side thought the development was an intended strategy of the Catholic Church to gain influence in Ukraine, as was the visit of Pope John Paul II to Kiev in the early summer of 2001. The church situation in Ukraine is still extremely complicated today. National aspects, which characterize the individual churches, play an important role.

Russian Orthodoxy, therefore, views the union as a method that not only decimates the Orthodox Church but also estranges the believers in their own tradition. That is why the argument, heard now and then from the side of the union, that the union is a model for a future unity between Rome and Orthodoxy, is not very convincing, since the present form of the Greek Catholic Church has an intimidating rather than attractive effect. The Russian Church accepted the fact that there is a Greek Catholic Church, and it accepts the right of the members of this church to receive pastoral care and have their own ecclesiastical identity. But it does not accept at all union decrees as a model for the future. In 1993, the Catholic Church and Orthodoxy agreed to accept the following principles within the framework of their official theological dialogue: "Uniatism" is no model for church unity; but today's Catholics of the Eastern Rite are an ecclesiastical reality and can claim their own identity.[3]

In Russia itself, there was a short-lived attempt at the beginning of the twentieth century to establish a Russian Catholic Church. Today, there are Catholic advocates who try again, misunderstanding the historical circumstances and disregarding the ecumenical principles of the Catholic Church. So far, their influence is small, and it is not expected to become greater. But they are certainly in a position to strengthen the perception of the Russian Church that the Catholic Church is an aggressive organization.

3. See the document of Balamand, passed by the Commission in 1993 in *Growth in Agreement, 1982-1998* II, ed. Harding Meyer and others (Grand Rapids: Eerdmans, 2001).

Ecumenical Relations

The relations between churches have substantially changed through the ecumenical movement. The movements for Faith and Order and for Life and Work, as well as the International Missionary Council, led to the establishment of the World Council of Churches in 1948. The Catholic Church opened itself at the Second Vatican Council (1962-65) to ecumenism, and since then, above all, is conducting a series of bilateral dialogues with other churches. Moreover, the cooperation of churches at the local level, in the parishes, has considerably improved through the ecumenical movement.

In the nineteenth century, the Russian Church conducted discussions with the Church of England as well as with the Old Catholic Church. Both were interesting partners in dialogue for Orthodoxy because they were "catholic" churches with the office of bishop and a similar view of sacraments, but they shared with Orthodoxy a rejection of Rome's claims of primacy. These contacts were interrupted by World War I and, above all, by the Revolution.

After 1917, Russian Orthodoxy could no longer maintain ecumenical relations, except through the theologians of the emigration, who were very active in such contacts. The Soviet government had no interest in relations with the church abroad. During World War II, in 1943, the Anglican archbishop of York was able to visit Moscow. But this meeting was, above all, political in order to thwart German propaganda in Russia through a demonstrative emphasis of religious freedom in Russia; German propaganda tried to win the favor of the population through liberal religious policy. At a conference in Moscow in 1948, with representatives of other Orthodox churches, especially from Communist-controlled countries, the ecumenical efforts, including the establishment of the World Council of Churches, were as harshly condemned as the Catholic attempts to expand.

But the attitude of the ROC to the World Council of Churches soon changed. The reasons are not undisputed. The authorities certainly noticed that the council was an instrument that could be used to present the positions of the Soviet Union abroad. But the church itself was interested in being able to make contact with other churches after decades of isolation, since relations to other churches had been de facto reduced to the other Orthodox churches in the Eastern Bloc. Moreover, this guaranteed that the ecumenical patriarch of Constantinople could not claim to be the only, or at least not the most important, representative of Orthodoxy.

The metropolitan of Leningrad and director of the Department for External Church Relations, Nikodim (Rotov), was the most important initiator of the ecumenical efforts of the Russian Church. He had a special proximity to the Catholic Church, symbolized by his death in 1978 during an audience with Pope John Paul I. Like all Russian hierarchs, he represented the official position of the USSR in political questions in the West. But it is known that he used the ecumenical contacts to ensure the theological exchange between his church and the Western churches as much as possible. After his return from ecumenical meetings, he used to report extensively to students at the theological academy in Leningrad so that they were informed about the situation in the West and in Western churches, as well as about the ecumenical developments, although that was not part of the official curriculum.

In bilateral ecumenical dialogues conducted by the Russian Church with many churches, among them also the Protestant churches in both German states, as well as with the Catholic Conference of Bishops in Germany, the Russian side set a high value on negotiating, always regarding a social ethical theme besides a theological topic in a narrower sense. The communiqués of such meetings, therefore, always stated something about the race of nuclear armaments, the idea of a globally based system of defense by missiles, or the Conference for Security and Cooperation in Europe. Today, the value of these dialogues and their statements is disputed. Whereas some considered them pure propaganda and qualified the Western partners in the dialogue as "useful idiots," others observed that these politically determined discussions were brought to a theological level. This different estimation can be found today in the East as well as in the West. It is clear that consideration of such topics was the condition for the Soviet authorities to permit the respective dialogues; the topics were not a part of the original agenda of the church. However, they included the "peace" theme, which, of course, has a deep theological dimension, in the theological agenda of Russian Orthodoxy as well as that of its partners in dialogue. It is also clear that the Western partners knew the situation of the Russian Church and that the dialogues on both sides were used to exchange information outside the daily agenda and the official program.

Besides the bilateral dialogues, the Russian Church was also engaged in multilateral ecumenism, above all, in the World Council of Churches and in the Conference of European Churches, founded in 1959-64. High-ranking representatives of the ROC had functions in these organizations. Metropolitan Alexiy (Ridiger) was president of the Conference of European Churches before his election to patriarch. Here, too, the Russian Church made an effort to determine the agenda of this organization and contributed something to make racism a theological topic in the 1970s. But Russian theologians also took part in the discussion of genuine theological themes such as the so-called Lima Process, resulting in the much noted document *Baptism, Eucharist, and Ministry*, published in 1982.

The end of the Soviet Union brought a noticeable cooling of the ecumenical engagement of Russian Orthodoxy. There are a number of explanations. Ecumenism needed no longer to serve as a way of enabling the representatives of the church to have contacts abroad. The authorities of the Russian Federation were no longer (or hardly ever, in any case) interested in the contacts of the Russian Church abroad, so there was no longer any restriction of its activities. The revival of the Greek Catholic Church in Ukraine, as well as the schisms of Ukrainian Orthodoxy, were further reasons for the restraint of Russian Orthodoxy, above all, regarding the Catholic Church. Ecumenical bodies continued to deal with topics in which Orthodoxy saw no room to move, such as the greater participation of women in church government and all the way to ordination, or the evaluation of homosexual unions. Finally, the Russian Church felt itself to be no longer properly represented in ecumenical governing bodies through the majority of churches in the tradition of the Reformation, and it demanded a structural reform of the World Council and of the Conference of European Churches. This was an issue not only for Russian Orthodoxy but also for all Orthodox churches. But the demands to withdraw completely from ecumenism, which also existed, did not prevail. Those who favored remaining argued that Orthodox theologians would be able to offer a witness of the true faith before representatives of other churches, an argument always used by Orthodox theologians for ecumenical engagement.

The relations with the Catholic Church deteriorated to a large extent. The situation in Ukraine was one reason; another was the creation of Roman Catholic ecclesiastical structures in the successor states of the Soviet Union, which had no Catholic hierarchy except in the predominantly Catholic Lithuania and Latvia. The culmination of these developments was the elevation of the existing four Catholic Apostolic Administrations in Russia to dioceses and the creation of a Catholic ecclesiastical province, "Russia," with the archbishopric in Moscow in February of 2002. Respect, to be sure, prevented the naming of the dioceses after the cities where the bishops resided, but after their cathedrals (such as St. Josef Diocese in Irkutsk). But the creation of dioceses happened de facto without proper consultation with the Orthodox Church. The result was a mutual public exchange of reproaches and accusations. The Russian side spoke of a Catholic proselytism that deliberately recruited Orthodox believers. Charitable institutions, it was said, were used for this purpose. The fact that the many religious orders active in Russia used the term "mission" in their name only strengthened the suspicion. On the Catholic side, most of these reproaches were rejected and the emphasis was put on problems the Catholic Church frequently encountered with Orthodox authorities.

In the subsequent debate, the Russian side argued with the idea of a "canonical territory." Accordingly, it would have jurisdiction to evangelize there. The Catholic Church could do pastoral care among its own members as well as among the descendants of Catholics, such as Poles and Lithuanians, who had been deported by Stalin to Siberia. Individual conversions should not be pursued but could be accepted. But the Catholic Church was not permitted to engage in a systematic mission, just as the Russian Church was not permitted to do so in Catholic territories. The Catholic side used the argument of religious liberty. After decades of atheism, there was a spiritual and religious vacuum. The various religious communities could exist side by side and should have the right to accept new believers. Subsequently, the Catholic Church tried to take the edge off the dispute, which had become complicated because the Russian authorities had refused to issue a residence permit to the Catholic bishop in Irkutsk, Jerzy Mazur, a Polish citizen, when he returned from a journey abroad. The ROC maintained it had nothing to do with the incident; the foreign office and President Putin declared that the refusal to issue an entry permit was justified.

An appropriate evaluation of the incidents is hardly possible. Both sides certainly acted badly. Some of the concrete reproaches of the Russian Church were admitted by the Catholic Church as mistakes; others were rejected. In the background, there is a differentiated assessment of religious liberty or canonical territory. The Russian Church spoke of "potentially Orthodox believers," meaning Russians who were not religious after the Soviet period but should in fact be Orthodox so that the Catholic Church should not be allowed to approach them. The Catholic Church of the country, which had amassed financial means in the first years after the end of Communism because of strong help from abroad, stressed that it could not and would not turn away seekers.

The disputes happened during the final years of Pope John Paul II, who probably could no longer deal with all the details. But it was important for the Russian Church that a Polish pope was involved, since the majority of the Catholic clergy and, above all, monastic orders in Russia were Poles. The problems with the Catholic Church are frequently interpreted in the light of the historical experiences of Russia with Poles. But it usually is not perceived that the Polish historical experiences with Russia and the Soviet Union are ignored. Relations seemed to improve after the election of Benedict XVI. The election of the German cardinal Ratzinger was acknowledged with satisfaction in the Russian Church, not because of his nationality but, above all, because of his reputation as a conservative theologian. Already in previous disputes about Catholic dioceses in Russia, one could notice in Russian statements a disappointment that in the fight against the evils of the time an expected confederate, the Catholic Church, had attacked Russian Orthodoxy from the rear. But now a pope heads the Catholic Church from whom no modernist aspirations could be expected and who, in all probability, would not sanction homosexuality or the ordination of women in the Catholic Church. Frequently, the Russian side demands an alliance between Orthodoxy and the Catholic Church in fighting liberalism, individualism, and subjectivism, which endanger Christian foundations and social values. Cardinal Ratzinger had spoken against these manifestations in his final sermon as cardinal at the opening of the conclave that elected him.

In the early summer of 2006, there was a conference of the Pontifical Council for Culture and the Department for External Church Relations of the ROC in Vienna, dealing with the topic "A Soul for Europe," the well-known saying of the former president of the European Union's commission, Jacques Delors, who called for a spiritual dimension to the process of European unification. This conference did not address the existing ecumenical successes in Europe, and the Ecumenical Council of Churches in Austria expressed its regret that the fully grown ecumenism was not considered and other churches had not been invited. This cooperation between the Catholic Church and the ROC was sometimes seen as the beginning of new relations between large churches. But the Protestant tradition and also the existing results of ecumenical contacts had been estimated as less important.

In 2005, the official theological dialogue between the Catholic Church and all of Orthodoxy received a new impetus so that, after a pause of six years, another meeting of the Common Commission could take place in September 2006. The ecumenical ice age seems to have come to an end. To be sure, the Russian Church's new openness for dialogue contributed to this, but changes in the other churches were the primary reason for this rather than a new attitude of Russian Orthodoxy.

CHAPTER TEN
....

Dissidence

⎯⎯⎯⎯⎯⎯

The Russian Church had almost always a solid system of theological ideas and doctrines as well as rules of conduct that affected the individual believers as well as the church itself regarding its relations to the outside. But there also always was religious dissidence; some people interpreted Christianity and its concrete form differently than did the church and were prepared to stand up for their convictions. Some such currents can be traced back to individuals. But they had no effect and remained historically unknown. Others had a great influence on Russian church history and became powerful movements, still existing today in the case of the Old Believers. It is no wonder that most of these movements are connected with the question of the church's relation to the West, that is, to Western influences. The (church-)political dissidence appears only in modern times. Other phenomena, like the Russian Church abroad, could also be described under this title. The rejection of communion with the patriarchal church, which was approved by the Soviet regime, is, of course, also an appearance of ecclesiastical disobedience.

Early Diverging Theological Developments

Movements of ecclesiastical opposition are only allusively recorded in the first centuries of the Russian Church. The main reason is the fact that the sources are destroyed and the opponents of these movements, which had finally prevailed, supply the only information about the doctrine of the respective group. But these sources must be read with a critical distance because the opponents were interested to present the respective group as maliciously and as heretically as possible.

The first movement that can be halfway historically assessed is the *Strigolniki*. The name probably means "the sheared ones" and points to a religious practice as an analogy to ecclesiastical consecration. The meaning "clothes trimmer" is also conceivable, pointing to the social origin. They emerged in Novgorod and in nearby Pskov toward the end of the fourteenth century. Apparently, the reason for their dissatisfaction was simony, and they carried on a controversy against unworthy priests. This not only was a question of morality and ecclesiastical discipline but also involved the certainty of salvation. How could the sacrament, necessary for salvation, be administered by priests who had sold their office or exercised it unworthily because they took money for their duties? Such considerations could generate basic questions about the office and external forms of the church. So also the sacraments, the veneration of icons, faith in the Trinity, monasticism, as well as a series of ecclesiastical phenomena became part of the criticism of the *Strigolniki*. But they could not prevail; their leaders were drowned in 1375.

It is difficult to say from where the ideas of the *Strigolniki* came. It is certain that criticism of priestly and episcopal abuse occurred more than occasionally in the Rus'. One surmised Western, perhaps Hussite, influence, because Novgorod had close relations to Lithuania. At the same time, various movements in the rest of Europe held similar views: the Bogomiles in Bulgaria, the *Krstiani* in Bosnia, the Cathari, Waldenses, and others in the West. Whether and how they influenced each other is disputed. But it is also conceivable that a Russian movement was connected to the aforementioned abuses. Novgorod, with its "democratic" structure, its urban districts, and its own autonomy and the right to elect priests, was predestined to become the place of origin for such a protest movement.

The situation of sources is somewhat better regarding the later, so-called Judaizers. They were probably called this because they denied the Trinity and considered the prophecies of the Old Testament not yet fulfilled. But the term was also used to describe deviating movements in the church as being under Jewish influence even though there was no reason for it. They appear in the late fifteenth century in Novgorod. There, they got into political quarrels: the Moscow Grand Prince Ivan III tried to integrate the city of Novgorod into the Moscow empire, and he finally succeeded after several campaigns. He especially acquired much real estate, but the ecclesiastical territory was still under the control of the rich Metropolitan Gennadiy in Novgorod. This is also the epoch of the quarrels between the two monastic parties, the nonpossessors and the Josephites.

The criticism of the Judaizers also seems to have ignited because of concrete abuses in the clergy and in the episcopacy. They turned against the hierarchy, the cult, and ecclesiastical property, and represented the idea of a simple, biblically founded life. They insisted on the teaching of the whole Bible (not only the parts used in worship), and they represented the idea of a "poor" church. Thus they came close, on the one hand, to the teaching of Nil Sorskiy and of the nonpossessors, but on the other hand, to the concrete intentions of the grand prince, who wanted to deprive the church of its property and also dispossess the Novgorod metropolitan. So it happened that, on one side, Joseph of Volokolamsk became the representative of the idea of a rich and strong church, together with Metropolitan Gennadiy, and on the other side were the Judaizers, Nil Sorskiy, and Grand Prince Ivan III.

As a consequence of this constellation of factors, the Judaizers in Novgorod were strongly persecuted, but, for the time being, the Judaizers in Moscow were tolerated. In 1490, they were condemned at a synod in Novgorod. The Moscow metropolitan, as well as Ivan III, was sympathetic toward them. Only when Gennadiy reproached the grand prince and the metropolitan for supporting heretics, and only after the death of the metropolitan, did a synod of 1504 in Moscow also condemn the Judaizers. Ivan III had become more conciliatory, probably because of common sense, but also after quarrels about the succession to the throne. The victors, Gennadiy and Joseph, demanded that the leaders of the heretics be executed by the secular authorities. Nil and the nonpossessors opposed this demand in polemical writings, but, in the end, the victorious side prevailed, and the leaders of the Judaizers were burned at the stake, their followers were severely persecuted, and the movement was eradicated.

A consequence of this quarrel was the rise of a theological polemics in which, above all, the two leaders of the monastic parties stood out. There is now in Russia a theological literature dealing with actual questions and taking clear positions. A further result was the first complete translation of the Bible into Old Russian, originating under Metropolitan Gennadiy between 1484 and 1499 as a consequence of a demand by the Judaizers. For a long time, this translation remained the basis for all further translations.

Finally, the most important theologian of the sixteenth century needs to be mentioned, Maksim Grek ("the Greek," 1470-1556). He came from Greece and studied in Florence, Italy. In 1502, he joined the Dominican order. Two years later he went to Mount Athos. In 1518, Grand Prince Vasiliy called him to Moscow to correct the translation of ecclesiastical texts. Maksim supported the nonpossessors (he himself had been, for some time, a member of a mendicant order) and probably also had a critical view of the Russian Church. After the fall of the metropolitan and the nomination of a successor, who belonged to the Josephites, the proposals for revision, made by Maksim in liturgical and theological texts because of deviations from the Greek originals, were rejected by two synods in 1525 and 1531. He himself was condemned. In 1548 he was dismissed but had to remain in Russia, namely, as prisoner of the Trinity Sergius Monastery, where he died in 1556. He has been venerated since the seventeenth century, but he was not canonized until 1988. His work has not yet been fully edited; he published, in the style of his time, polemics against Jews, Muslims, Armenians, and Latins, without leaving behind any systematic theological presentation.

Maksim Grek is the most prominent example of a victim of the ecclesiastical opposition to influences from Greece. A good hundred years later, the same controversy was to provide for a long-enduring schism.

The Old Believers

The availability of printing and the improved relations with the Greek Church after the elevation to a patriarchate made the necessity of revising and unifying the liturgical books more urgent since there were numerous mistranslations and abuses. The resistance, which again and again appeared against all efforts to change what was handed down, frequently came from the monks. They wanted to fasten contents of faith to doctrinal formulae, an expression of a certain traditionalism that did not reflect about faith but, above all, simply handed it on. A change of forms would then have to mean a change of faith. In addition, there was the new self-consciousness of the state that had increased its power and claimed to be the leading power in Orthodoxy and could prevail against the ever stronger Greek influences.

This situation, as well as the growing influence from Ukraine, made Patriarch Nikon (1652-66) decide to order a reform of the liturgical books, after previously unsuccessful attempts, and to remove other liturgical abuses. In addition, he wanted to adjust Russian customs to Greek ones. Various Greek patriarchs and metropolitans also contributed to the decision because they had been in Moscow and had noticed the various improper developments. The still customary "parallel singing," that is, the simultaneous singing of various parts of the liturgy by various choirs, done to shorten the worship service, was to be totally prohibited; the Hundred-Chapter Synod of 1551 already had prohibited it, but without complete success.

In other questions, however, the measures of Nikon of 1653 contradicted the Hundred-Chapter Synod: the sign of the cross was no longer made with two fingers, but now with three; processions around the church were to be done in the direction opposite to the course of the sun instead of with the sun; the name Jesus was to be spelled "Iisus," no longer "Isus," and the Hallelujah was to be sung three times at specific parts of the liturgy, not twice. There were justifications for all these changes, as well as for the existing practice; they appeared to be convincing and irrefutable to the representatives of the respective trends. The two fingers in the old sign of the cross symbolize the two natures in Jesus Christ; the three fingers symbolize the three divine persons. But to opponents of the reforms the three fingers meant a "satanic Trinity." Such arguments were not the primary issue, but how one could find a way back to the unchanged tradition of the beginnings, namely, by retaining old "Russian" customs that, as was surmised, represented the original forms taken over by the Greeks, or adjusting to the contemporary Greek (and thus the entire) Orthodox Church. The Hundred-Chapter Synod codified the "Russian" customs. But after the elevation to patriarchy and the reconciliation with Greek Orthodoxy, this decision seemed to be obsolete.

A group of priests opposed the decision of Nikon; Nikon himself had once belonged to this group, which was later called a "circle of enthusiasts." The influential father confessor of the tsar, Stefan Vonifatev, and the arch-priests Ivan Neronov and Avvakum also belonged to it. Avvakum (ca. 1620-82) became the most renowned representative of the Old Believers because of his publications, especially his autobiography. Other members of this informal circle had tried in previous years to push back the growing influence of the Greek traditions in favor of the traditions of the Hundred-Chapter Synod. For this purpose, an appeal was made, above all, to theologians from Kiev. But Kiev had always been connected with Constantinople. So some publications appeared that were to become highly esteemed later because they were older than the reforms of Nikon. But occasionally Greek and also Western influences can be found in these books.

Under Nikon, the direct Greek influence increased and the Ukrainian influence decreased. When opposition to the measures became noisy in the circle of enthusiasts, the patriarch reacted harshly — Neronov was dismissed from his office and imprisoned in a monastery; although Avvakum remained a priest, he was deported to Siberia. In the subsequent years, the new measures were passed at synods at which Greek bishops, who were present in Moscow, played an important role. But the opposition could no longer be slowed down. Avvakum agitated also in exile against the reforms, worked in Moscow through messengers and correspondence, and was exiled still farther to the east, to the Amur River. In 1664, he was brought back to Moscow after the patriarch's influence with the tsar had waned. But since he continued to defend the old rite, he was excommunicated and again exiled, first in 1666 and again in 1667, after Nikon's dismissal. This excommunication excluded him from the church. He, in turn, excommunicated the patriarch and the church that supported him, thus creating de facto an alternative church. In 1682, Avvakum was finally burned at the stake because he continued to fight against the reforms in his writings. His autobiography is not only a valuable source for the quarrel about the imperial reform but also a first-rate social-historical and literary witness.[1]

Avvakum would have been a single, almost forgotten fighter against the reforms if they had not been broadly rejected. Many joined the schism (raskol in Russian, thus also the old designation Raskolniki), and the resistance against the reforms spread widely in the land, above all, in the north and in the monasteries. The quarrels cost thousands of lives, be it through massive suicides (above all, through suicide by fire) committed by the movement to avoid capture by state troops. The Solovetskiy Monastery on an island in the White Sea withstood a siege of eight years by tsarist troops, but finally was conquered, resulting in the death of hundreds of monks and civilians. Despite these measures and a strict persecution, the "Old Believers" or "Old Ritualists" were able to survive. Many emigrated to Siberia and established settlements that partly still exist today, and to Alaska even farther away. Other remote territories, above all,

---

1. *Archpriest Avvakum: The Life Written by Himself,* Michigan Slavic Translations (Ann Arbor: University of Michigan Press, 1979).

in the north of the country, were chosen as places of settlement. Since relatively many acknowledged the old rite, the movement could not be eliminated. Although some members of the upper class could also be found among the Old Believers, later it consisted, above all, of simple people, peasants, and craftsmen as well as merchants. The Old Believers attained great economic significance.

There are many reasons why such a lasting social movement arose from the resistance against some ecclesiastical reforms. The ecclesiastical-theological significance must not be overestimated, but it was the three-finger sign of the cross that became the symbol of the reforms and affected every Christian every day. It was, therefore, not a reform that only changed priestly actions in the liturgy but it affected the entire church and every individual. Moreover, one must not overlook the atmosphere of eschatological end-time expectations of the epoch, linked often with apocalyptical ideas. So the interpretation that the tsar or the patriarch was the Antichrist and the Old Believers were the holy remnant that does not yield, could easily succeed. When the expectation was not fulfilled, that is, when the "Antichrist" Peter I died and world history did not end, there appeared new interpretations, which often were connected with schisms.

It is noteworthy that the quarrels did not deal with questions of faith in a narrower sense but with liturgical details. But liturgical symbols are inseparably connected with contents, and a change of the external sign then also means a change of the faith thus symbolized. If the two fingers of the sign of the cross mean the two natures of Christ, then it is not possible, according to this understanding, to make another sign of the cross. For Orthodox thinking, the rite was much more than just an external sign.

Besides these religious reasons there also were social ones that affected, above all, the peasants and, in many ways, created a common dissatisfaction with the innovations, especially those from the West. In Russia, the seventeenth century was marked by a series of revolts, and the movement against the reform could, for the time being, present itself to the state as one revolt in a series. Moreover, in the beginning, the Old Believers were also not a structured and organized movement. There were different centers of the resistance that united with a common concern. Despite the strict measures of persecution by the state, these centers were able to stay in touch with each other through messengers and itinerant monks and then organize slowly, even though there never was a totally united church of the Old Believers.

In the subsequent centuries, the Old Believers were again and again persecuted by the state and not acknowledged by the church. Under Peter I, the strict persecutions relaxed, only to be taken up again later. Not until the Edict of Toleration in 1905 was freedom of religion granted to the Old Believers in Russia. They suffered as much under the Soviet measures of persecution as did the patriarchal church; in 1971, the latter lifted the still existing anathema against them. The Old Believers still use today the liturgy from the time before the reforms. They also preserved their own style in the painting of icons, since Avvakum had already carried on a controversy against Western influences.

There were numerous schisms among the Old Believers.[2] No bishop joined them, so they could not ordain priests. So one part of the Old Believers recruited (sometimes even systematically) priests from the patriarchal church. This group was called the "Priestlies" (*popovcy* in Russian) because they basically acknowledged the priesthood. In the nineteenth century, there was an Orthodox bishop in the Hapsburg Empire who ordained Old Believer bishops and eventually established a hierarchy. The Priestlies still exist today and are the largest group. Their center is in Moscow, and they have some bishops, above all, in the CIS. The number of believers is estimated to be about 400,000, but such specifications must be considered with great caution. The group of "those with deserted priests" (an outside designation, *beglopopovcy* in Russian) is supposed to be just as large. They did not acknowledge the hierarchy of the Priestlies and received their own bishops only through conversion in the twentieth century. In the meantime, they elevated their church to a patriarchy. The two churches have bad relations with each other. The "unity believers" *(yedinovertsy)* are a group that has existed since the early nineteenth century and belongs to the patriarchal church; but they kept the old rites. They can be characterized as Old Believers on the basis of their rite, but not with respect to jurisdiction. There is also a Church of Old Believers in Romania; it had fled there from the persecution in Russia.

The second main group is the "Priestless" *(bespopovcy)*, who believed the priesthood ended after the first generation of Old Believer priests became extinct. This, too, was interpreted as proof that the end time had begun. After that, there could only be the sacraments of baptism and of penance (both administered by laymen in cases of emergency), and of the Eucharist (through preconsecrated gifts). The Priestless split into many

2. Detailed presentation in Peter Hauptmann, *Russlands Altgläubige* (Göttingen: Vandenhoeck & Ruprecht, 2005).

groups. Some of them did not marry because of the lack of the sacrament of marriage — they demanded abstinence and soon died out. Others secularized marriage and enabled the continued existence of the group. Among some of them, a kind of prayer room served as a church building, but still with a wall of icons as a closure of the room. From some groups, sects developed. Since there was no hierarchy, the Priestless had a parochial organization, and some parishes consolidated. The number and status of the Priestless can hardly be reliably established. In Russia, there are more than a hundred parishes without priests, and others are in the Baltic States, above all, in Latvia.

The Old Believers had, and still have, a great internal consistency. Many Russian families of merchants emerged from them. The economic success also was linked to the frequently practiced abstention from alcohol and to the great discipline within the group. The fact that the recruiting of priests from the patriarchal church was very often successful is also a sign of the economic possibilities among the Old Believers. Their parishes could provide a secure future for the sons of priests born later.

Russian Sects

Since the seventeenth century, sects have been increasing in Russia. This is, in part, a consequence of the schism of the Old Believers, from whom some sects developed. But this phenomenon is also linked to the rejection of a close proximity between church and state. Resistance against such a proximity manifested itself in two ways. On the one hand, there was the form of an increased spirituality within the church, averting ecclesiastical structures, as evidenced in the Startsy. The other form in which the rejection of such proximity could be expressed was movements outside the church. They often originated in a climate of end-time speculations and were mostly marked by extreme forms of asceticism, as well as frequently by ideas of incarnation. Some of them are sketched here. But the sects coming from the West, which still exist in Russia today, are not presented here.

The Khlysts named themselves "people of God." The origin of the name is unclear; it can mean "flagellants." They probably originated from Old Believers without priests in the seventeenth century. Speculations about their Gnostic or Oriental roots cannot be maintained. Their basic witness is the existence of ever new incarnations of God, Jesus Christ,

Mary, the apostles, and prophets in Russian individuals. Their founder, Danila Filippov, claimed to be God Sabaoth and appointed a peasant as Christ and a peasant woman as Mother of God. Ever since, there were always new embodiments of Christ and Mary that led to the establishment of new communities. The Khlysts spread extensively. Their worship services included liturgical dancing and singing that intensified into ecstasy. These worship services were preceded by a strict abstinence from food and sex (thus also the designation "Fasters," *postniki*). Like other sects, the Khlysts tried to protect themselves from the authorities by living inconspicuously and participating in the social life of the Orthodox Church. That is why there were numerous members in monasteries. After the eighteenth century, the Khlysts were severely persecuted.

In the nineteenth century, the Khlysts disintegrated into numerous groups, some of which tried to realize the kingdom of God on earth and, accordingly, called themselves "Israel" or "New Israel." Before the First World War, the Khlysts had about 40,000 members. The Soviet regime countenanced Khlystianism because of its presumably revolutionary potential. But the persecution began after 1925. In the 1960s, there were still remnants of this community. It is not clear whether Khlysts still exist today.

At the end of the eighteenth century, the Skoptsy ("those who cut themselves," or "white doves," as they called themselves) split from the Khlysts. They realized a radical sexual abstinence through castration in order to attain salvation through such purity. In the background was the idea of the church as a community of those who are pure and sinless. Their cult was similar to that of the Khlysts, but they did not know the idea of the repeated incarnation; they understood their founder as the Christ of the end time and as Tsar Peter III. The idea of self-mutilation ("baptism by fire") is based on Matthew 19:12 and on the idea that sexuality has to do with sin and death. The Skoptsy were severely persecuted by the Russian authorities, and therefore they had to live in retreat and with a secret discipline. They probably became extinct in the middle of the final third of the twentieth century.

Today, there are still small groups of Dukhobors ("fighters of the Spirit," "spiritual Christians" as self-designation) and a group, originating with them, known as Molokans ("milk drinkers"). These are groups that reject the tradition of the church and also do not know the ascetic rigorism of the aforementioned groups. The Dukhobors do not acknowledge any icons, written documents of faith (including the Bible), sacraments, or a redemption through Jesus Christ. Similar to some Western revival movements, they believe that Christ is realized in every individual who has experienced an inner revelation. They confess the indwelling of the Holy Spirit in every individual. Their ethical model is the Sermon on the Mount. However, it is difficult to apprehend their teaching in a systematic manner. In 1917, there were still about 20,000 Dukhobors; the present number is not known.

The Molokans derive their name from the fact that they drink milk during Lent, which is prohibited in the Orthodox tradition. Their teaching is very similar to that of the Dukhobors, but is more rationalized. The Bible is the source of revelation, whereas the ecumenical councils falsified the teaching of Scripture. Their teachings became widely known through many forced resettlements. They also disintegrated into many groups that developed their own teachings and liturgical forms.

These sects come from the Russian Orthodox tradition. They are, as is evident in their beliefs, either apocalyptically or rationalistically oriented, but come from the Russian Church and use (although sometimes with demarcations) what they find in its tradition. According to the nature of things, the sects are not well researched, and often there are no sources. But regarding questions of ecclesiastical dissidence, it would be interesting to search for elements of continuity and discontinuity that always provide a framework for such phenomena.

After the end of the Soviet Union, many new religious movements originated. They often appeared with great public attention. They, too, are frequently marked by extreme forms and views, again through the central role of a leading personality. The Vissarion Group, named after the pseudonym of their founder in Siberia, and the White Fraternity are probably the best-known sects. But it is hardly possible to say anything reliable about them. Time will tell whether these groups can endure.

Religious Dissenters in the USSR

The concluding section is dedicated to a phenomenon that probably comes first to mind with the term "dissident": people who disagree with the ideology and practice of the Communist system. They articulate another way of thinking, as dissenters, without resisting the system by force. Names like Alexander Solzhenitsyn and Andrey Sakharov stand in for many others who put up with privations, deportation, exile, imprison-

CROSS AND KREMLIN

ment, and even death. The commitment to human rights also meant a commitment to religious freedom, even though many dissenters were personally not religious. But some did get into conflict with the state because of their religious convictions. It is clear that this had to mean a simultaneous conflict with the patriarchal church, since it basically was loyal to the state.

In the years after the declaration of loyalty by Metropolitan Sergiy (Stragorodskiy) in 1927, numerous Christians did not accept such a step and no longer acknowledged the patriarchal church. They had to organize in secret and so were called the "Catacomb Church"; their self-designation was "True Orthodox Church." There were, indeed, attempts to establish a connection with individual parishes, but there probably never was a unified ecclesiastical organization. The degree of resistance against the regime was highly varied. But often apocalyptic ideas played an important role, according to which the end time seemed to have begun with the Soviet Union (or after concrete measures of persecution). The members of these groups suffered severe persecution. Since there was no bishop who supported them after the Second World War, the priests of the first generation gradually died out. Frequently, groups now called themselves "True Orthodox Christians" and organized as prayer groups or lay circles, but without contact with the patriarchal church. It cannot be determined how many people belonged to such groups. But they existed until the end of the USSR. It is known that other groups had an informal link with the patriarchal church, for example, women who took an oath of virginity before a bishop, lived with other women in a residence, and worked in hospitals. This form of monasticism was really illegal but occurred with the approval of the bishop.

After the church began cooperating with the state in 1945, more cases of ecclesiastical dissidence appeared. The first was the open letter of the Moscow priests Nikolay Eshliman and Gleb Yakunin to Patriarch Alexiy I (Simanskiy), written in 1965. Both priests denounced the growing closings of churches and other abuses and blamed church leadership for not confronting the secular authorities and becoming engaged for the freedom of the church. Patriarch Alexiy suspended both priests and demanded in a letter that all bishops prohibit such expressions of opinion. This was the method with which the church reacted also in other cases. In no known case did the church stand on the side of the dissenters against the state. Two years later, Archbishop Yermogen (Golubev), who had been sent into retirement because of his attitude, sent a "petition" to the patriarch, complaining about the church structure and the way of electing a bishop because they did not abide by the decision of the local council of 1917. Here, too, the synod did not support the bishop but regretted and condemned his attitude. Yermogen was forced to live in a monastery until his death in 1978.

The ecclesiastical dissidence received an important impulse through the "Fasting Letter," sent in the spring of 1974 by the writer Alexander Solzhenitsyn, who had lost his citizenship, to Patriarch Pimen (Izvekov). In plain words, he criticized the head of the church for permitting atheists to control the church and for making too many concessions to the state. In the subsequent years the dissidence increased, and the state reacted with increased persecution after 1979. Among the dissenters, who were almost all urban intellectuals who had become believers in their youth or as adults, two directions emerged: a rather liberal one, which reflected the common discussion of human rights, and a rather national one, which occasionally even sounded anti-Semitic. Although the liberal one became more important, the existence of the other indicated that the coalition between nationally oriented Communists and people in the church, sometimes visible today, had already found its roots here.

The engagement of the Russian Church in the ecumenical movement provided dissenters with the opportunity to gain international attention for their concerns. At the assembly of the World Council of Churches in 1975 in Nairobi, the delegation of the ROC got into difficulties because two dissenters, the priest Yakunin and the layman Lev Regelson, had written a letter that was published in the newspaper of the conference, denouncing the Soviet politics of religion.[3] Although the assembly did not deal officially with the letter because it was not a proposal of a member church, there was an intense discussion about the question at events outside the official program. The delegates of the Russian Church, who reacted after three days with an official response, retreated to a formal position. They claimed that only a few isolated and false voices were involved, that in the USSR one was only punished for violating laws, not for religious engagements; the issue is to be seen in relation to the conference on security and cooperation in Europe in the same year in Helsinki where the Soviet Union had subscribed to "Basket 3," that is, the acknowledgment of human rights. In 1979, Yakunin and Regelson were ar-

3. See the letter and the reaction of the church leadership in David Kelly, "Nairobi: A Door Opened," in *Religion in Communist Lands* 4 (1976): 4-17.

rested. Yakunin was sentenced to five years in a labor camp and to five more years in exile.

In the USSR, illegal groups and circles were formed, dealing with religious themes. The dissenter Tatyana Goricheva became famous in the West and had belonged to such a group in Leningrad until her expulsion in 1980. There also were circles of study whose members were explicitly loyal to Christianity. But they attached less significance to attending the liturgy than to reading religious and philosophical writings, as well as discussing them. Some of these groups published illegal writings and chronicles. In 1976, a Committee for the Defense of Believers in the USSR was founded. It existed for several years and succeeded in smuggling many documents to the West. But there always was the danger of discovery by the KGB. Dissenters who walked into the trap of the authorities were usually sentenced to years in a camp. The usual charge in such cases was "anti-Soviet propaganda."

The Moscow priest Dmitriy Dudko was known for his critical remarks in sermons and publications. This was an illegal act, but it attracted many young people. Although he was repeatedly transferred, he (unlike other clergy dissenters) remained in his office and was not suspended. That is why his arrest in 1980 was a surprise. After a few months, Soviet television transmitted his declaration of repentance, which he obviously had been forced to make. He could continue his function as a priest and, with restrictions, also do his pastoral duties. A few years later, *perestroika* began, and dissenters were no longer persecuted. Dudko, who died in 2004, was in his final years an opponent of the political and social development in Russia. He made positive comments about Stalin and supported the Communist Party. He obviously seemed to view the development toward a pluralistic and open society as more threatening than a system that looked stable from the outside, even though it was repressive.

The so-called *samizdat* (private publication by an author) was an important medium for dissenting groups and thus also for religious dissent. The term means the copying and distribution of writings in an informal manner, mostly primitive transcripts of books from the West, or literature originating in the country. The *samizdat* represented a way to spread ideas in the country from the Soviet underground.

The contact with like-minded people in the West was always important for the dissenters. Religious broadcasts and news were transmitted by radio, especially from the American station Radio Liberty in Munich.

Many travelers from the West, above all, church groups, brought Bibles into Russia. Conversely, some documents could reach the West from the Soviet Union through travelers or other channels.

The religious dissenters helped to maintain the consciousness of the suppression of the church in the West. They were a special thorn in the flesh of the Soviet authorities because of their loyalty to the patriarchal church. But they also were a problem for the churches in the West because, on the one hand, one wanted to help those who were persecuted for their religion but, on the other hand, the official Russian representatives of Russian Orthodoxy, when asked about dissenters, always disclaimed persecution for religious reasons. This was a difficult situation especially for the ecumenical governing boards, which did not always act wisely and, above all, let down the dissenters.

After the end of the Soviet Union, some dissenters became reconciled with their church while others moved away from it. Today, there is no suppression of religious dissidence by secular authorities in Russia. The topic has different dimensions after the end of Communism. But the importance of the anti-Soviet religious dissenters remains.

Chronological Table

839	First mention of the name *Rhos.*
860-1240	**Kievan Rus'**
988	"Baptism of the Rus'" under Grand Prince Vladimir.
11th century	Flowering period of the Rus' under Grand Prince Yaroslav.
1037	Beginning of the building of Saint Sophia Cathedral in Kiev.
1051	The first Slavic metropolitan of Kiev, Ilarion.
1113	Origin of Nestor's Chronicle.
1169	Grand Prince Andrey Bogoljubskiy conquers Kiev. The decay of the Rus' begins.
1223	Tartar tribes from the Asian steppe threaten the Rus'.
1240	Battle on the Neva. Prince Alexander Nevskiy defeats the Swedes.
1240-1340	**Early Period of Mongol Rule**
1240	The Khan of the Tartars, Batu, conquers Kiev and subjugates the southwestern Russian principalities.
1242	Alexander Nevskiy defeats the army of the German Teutonic Knights.
1299	Emigration of Metropolitan Maksim from Kiev to Vladimir.
1328	The grand prince rank is permanently connected with Moscow. The metropolitan moves his residence to Moscow.

Chronological Table

1340-1689	**The Moscow Epoch**
1380	Battle on the Field of Snipes. Dmitriy Donskoy defeats the Tartars.
About 1400	Flowering of icon painting (Feofan Grek, Andrey Rublev).
1459	Autocephaly. The Russian Church declares its independence.
1462	Ivan III becomes Grand Prince. Formal end of Tartar rule. Suspension of tributes.
1547	Metropolitan Makariy crowns Ivan IV ("the Terrible") tsar and autocrat of Russia.
1551	The Hundred-Chapter Synod introduces many reforms, above all, in the realm of liturgy.
1589	Elevation of the metropolitanate of Moscow to the patriarchy.
1595-96	Union of Brest. Orthodox bishops in Poland-Lithuania place themselves under Rome and form a Greek Catholic ("uniate") Church.
1598-1613	"Time of Troubles." The death of Tsar Fedor Ivanovich in 1598 ends the dynasty of the Ryurikids. In 1613, Tsar Mikhail starts the rule of the Romanovs.
1632	Establishment of "Kiev College" *(Collegium Kioviense)* in Kiev.
1653	Reform of the liturgy under Patriarch Nikon.
1666-67	The Great Moscow Council passes an improvement of the Rites. The Old Believers (Old Ritualists) split from the church, led by the priest Avvakum.
1667	Kiev and the left bank (eastern) Ukraine fall to Russia.
1689-1917	**From Peter I to the End of the Epoch of the Tsars**
1689	Accession of Peter I ("the Great"). Numerous reforms in church and state.
1721	Dissolution of the patriarchy. Installation of the Holy Synod as governing body.
1722-24	Reform of the monasteries.
1762	Secularization of ecclesiastical property. Termination of monasteries.
1905	Revolution. Edict of Toleration for other denominations and religions.

1917-91	**Soviet Russia**
1917	"Bourgeois Revolution" in February and Bolshevist October Revolution.
1917-18	Local council of the Orthodox Church.
1917, Nov. 4	Restitution of the patriarchy. Metropolitan Tikhon becomes new patriarch.
1917, Dec. 2	Secularization of the ecclesiastical territory.
1918, Jan.	Metropolitan Vladimir of Kiev is the first martyr by shooting. Beginning of the bloody persecution of the church.
1918, Jan. 20	"Decree on Freedom of Conscience." Separation of state and church.
1921	Constitution of the "Karlovtsi Synod."
1923	Declaration of Repentance of Patriarch Tikhon.
1925	Death of Patriarch Tikhon. No immediate new election is possible.
1927	Joseph Stalin assumes power. Declaration of loyalty to the Soviet Union by Metropolitan Sergiy.
1941, Jun. 20	German army assaults the USSR.
1943	Relaxation of the politics of religion. Stalin uses the church to strengthen the patriotic resistance against the German occupation. The new election of a patriarch is granted.
1946	"Pseudo-Council of Lviv." The Greek Catholic Church is placed under the authority of the patriarch of Moscow.
1956	"Thaw." De-Stalinization begins under Nikita Khrushchev.
1961	ROC joins the World Council of Churches.
1988	Millennium of the baptism of the Rus'. Turn in church politics under Gorbachev.
1990	Alexiy II (Ridiger) is elected patriarch.
1991	Dissolution of the USSR.
1991-	**Russia after the End of the USSR**
2000	"Social Doctrine" of the Russian Orthodox Church.
2002, Feb.	Establishment of a Roman Catholic ecclesiastical province with four dioceses. Tensions in the relations between the ROC and the Catholic Church.
2007, May	Reunion of the ROC with the church abroad.
2009	Election of Patriarch Kirill (Gundyayev).

Bibliography

Beck, H. G. *Das byzantinische Jahrtausend.* Munich: C. H. Beck, 1978.

Behrens, Kathrin. *Die russische Orthodoxe Kirche: Segen für die "neuen Zaren"? Religion und Politik im postsowjetischen Russland (1991-2000).* Paderborn: Schöningh, 2002.

Bulgakov, Sergius. *Icons and the Name of God.* Translated by Boris Jakim. Grand Rapids and Cambridge, UK: Eerdmans, 2012.

————. *Relics and Miracles: Two Theological Essays.* Translated by Boris Jakim. Grand Rapids and Cambridge, UK: Eerdmans, 2012.

Davis, Nathaniel. *A Long Walk to Church: A Contemporary History of Russian Orthodoxy.* Boulder, Colo.: Westview Press, 1995.

Diedrich, Hans-Christian, and others, eds. *Das Gute behaltet. Kirchen und religiöse Gemeinschaften in der Sowjetunion und ihren Nachfolgestaaten.* Erlangen: Martin-Luther-Bund, 1996.

Ellis, Jane. *The Russian Orthodox Church: A Contemporary History.* London and Sydney: Croom Helm, 1986.

Felmy, K. Chr., and others, eds. *Tausend Jahre Christentum in Russland.* Göttingen: Vandenhoeck & Ruprecht, 1988.

Freeze, Gregory, ed. *Russia: A History.* Oxford and New York: Oxford University Press, 1997.

Goerdt, Wilhelm. *Russische Philosophie. Zugänge und Durchblicke.* Freiburg and Munich: Karl Alber, 1984.

Hauptmann, Peter. *Russlands Altgläubige.* Göttingen: Vandenhoeck & Ruprecht, 2005.

Hauptmann, Peter, and Gerd Stricker, eds. *Die Orthodoxe Kirche in Russland.*

Dokumente ihrer Geschichte (860-1980). Göttingen: Vandenhoeck & Ruprecht, 1988.

Hösch, Edgar. *Geschichte Russlands. Vom Kiever Reich bis zum Verfall des Sowjetimperiums*. Stuttgart, Berlin, and Cologne: Kohlhammer, 1996.

Hösch, Edgar, and Hans-Jürgen Grabmüller. *Daten der russischen Geschichte. Von den Anfängen bis 1917*. Munich: DTV, 1981.

Kappeler, Andreas. *Russland als Vielvölkerreich*. Munich: C. H. Beck, 1992.

―――. *Russische Geschichte*. Munich: C. H. Beck, 1997.

Korpela, Jukka. *Prince, Saint, and Apostle: Prince Vladimir Svjatoslavic of Kiev, His Posthumous Life, and the Religious Legitimization of the Russian Great Power*. Wiesbaden: Harrassowitz, 2001.

Metropolitan Pitirim von Volokolamsk and Jurjev, eds. *Die Russische Orthodoxe Kirche*. New York: de Gruyter, Evangelisches Verlagswerk, 1988.

Müller, Ludolf. *Die Taufe Russlands. Die Frühgeschichte des russischen Christentums bis zum Jahre 988*. Munich: Wewel, 1987.

Onasch, Konrad. *Grundzüge der russischen Kirchengeschichte*. Göttingen: Vandenhoeck & Ruprecht, 1967.

Payer, Alja, and Gottfried Glassner. *Bibliographie der deutschsprachigen Literatur über das Christentum in Russland und Nachfolgestaaten der UdSSR (1986-1993)*. Munich: Eigenverlag des Stiftes Melk, 1998.

Podskalsky, Gerhard. *Christentum und theologische Literatur in der Kiever Rus' (988-1237)*. Munich: C. H. Beck, 1982.

Pospielovsky, Dimitry. *The Russian Church under the Soviet Regime, 1917-1982*. 2 vols. Crestwood, N.Y.: St. Vladimir's Seminary Press, 1984.

Scheliha, Wolfram von. *Russland und die orthodoxe Universalkirche in der Patriarchatsperiode, 1589-1721*. Wiesbaden: Harrassowitz, 2004.

Schenk, Frithjof B. *Aleksandr Nevskij. Heiliger, Fürst, Nationalheld. Eine Erinnerungsfigur im russischen kulturellen Gedächtnis (1262-2000)*. Cologne, Weimar, Vienna: Böhlau, 2004.

Schulz, Günter. *Das Landeskonzil der Orthodoxen Kirche in Russland 1917-18. Ein unbekanntes Reformpotential*. Göttingen: Vandenhoeck & Ruprecht, 1995.

Schulz, Günter, Gisela A. Schröder, and C. Timm Richter. *Bolschewistische Herrschaft und Orthodoxe Kirche in Russland. Das Landeskonzil 1917-18. Quellen und Analysen*. Münster: LIT, 2005.

Smolitsch, Igor. *Russisches Mönchtum. Entstehung, Entwicklung und Wesen 988-1917*. Würzburg: Augustinus Verlag, 1953.

―――. *Leben und Lehren der Starzen. Der Weg zum vollkommenen Leben*. Freiburg, Basel, and Vienna: Herder, 1988.

————. *Geschiche der russischen Kirche.* Vol. 1, Leiden: Brill, 1964. Vol. 2, Wiesbaden: Harrassowitz, 1991.

Stökl, Günther. *Russische Geschichte von den Anfängen bis zur Gegenwart.* Stuttgart: Kröner, 1997.

Stricker, Gerd. *Religion in Russland. Darstellung und Daten zu Geschichte und Gegenwart.* Gütersloh: Gütersloher Verlagshaus, 1993.

Theising, Joseph, and Rudolf Uertz, eds. *Die Grundlagen der Sozialdoktrin der Russisch-Orthodoxen Kirche. Deutsche Übersetzung mit Einführung und Kommentar.* St. Augustin: Konrad-Adenauer-Stiftung, 2001.

Torke, Hans-Joachim J. *Einführung in die Geschichte Russlands.* Munich: C. H. Beck, 1997.

Vulpius, Ricarda. *Nationalisierung der Religion. Russifizierungspolitik und ukrainische Nationsbildung 1860-1920.* Wiesbaden: Harrassowitz, 2005.

Willems, Joachim. *Religiöse Bildung in Russlands Schulen. Orthodoxie, nationale Identität und die Positionalität des Faches "Grundlagen orthodoxer Literatur"* (OPK). Münster: Lit, 2006.

Internet

Web site of the Russian Patriarchate (in Russian):

www.patriarchia.ru/

Web site of the Department for External Church Relations (in English):

https://mospat.ru/en/

E-mail service with news on churches in Eastern Europe (German and English):

www.kirchen-in-osteuropa.de/

Index of Persons

Index of Places

Alexandria, 18, 58
Antioch, 18, 58

Bad Ems, 48
Baden-Baden, 48
Bad Homburg, 48
Belgrade, 49
Boston, 106
Byzantium, 16, 34, 57, 58, 71, 92, 93-94. *See also* Byzantium in the subject index

Carlsbad (Karlovy Vary), 49
Constantinople, 8, 9, 15, 16, 18, 54, 56, 58, 71, 140. *See also* Constantinople in the subject index

Edinburgh, 106

Florence, 136, 141, 152

Galich (Halich), 11, 38, 39, 53, 54

Harvard, 106
Hokkaido, 45

Ingelheim, 35
Irkutsk, 146, 147

Jerusalem, 18, 58, 119

Karlovy Vary. *See* Carlsbad
Kazan, 44, 45, 97
Kiev, 7, 8, 11, 14, 15, 35, 38, 40, 41, 53, 54, 55, 60, 110, 112. *See also* Kiev in the subject index

Lausanne, 106
Leningrad, 162
Lviv, 54, 60

Moscow, 2, 4, 7, 8, 11, 14-18, 20, 39-42, 54, 56, 57, 65, 66, 73, 75, 77, 85, 97, 102, 105, 110, 114, 117, 129, 137, 141, 144, 146, 151-54, 156. *See also* Moscow in the subject index
Munich, 49, 162

New York, 45, 50, 106
Novgorod, 11, 14, 39, 40

Oxford, 106

Paris, 50, 102, 103, 105, 106, 138
Princeton, 106
Pskov, 150

Rome, 16, 21, 38, 61, 77, 141, 142. *See also* Rome in the subject index

San Francisco, 45

Index of Subjects

Academy: of Kazan, 44, 97; of Kiev, 21, 95, 97, 112; of Leningrad and Zagorsk, 104, 145; of Moscow, 22, 62, 98, 99; in St. Petersburg, 97
Alaska, 44, 45
Anarchism, Russian, 104
Andrew's Legend, 37
Armenia, 5, 68
Asceticism, 74, 110-14, 123, 124
Assyrian Church, 45
Atheism, 83, 89
Athos, Mount, 109, 115, 118
Autocephaly (of the Russian Orthodox Church), 16, 55

Battle on the Field of Snipes, 12
Belarus, 68, 141
Bolsheviki, Bolsheviks, 25, 27, 28, 48, 49, 66, 80, 98
Brezhnev era, 31
Byzantium: conflicts with, 35; influence of, 10; legacy of, 16, 90, 93; literature, 93, 94; significance, 73. *See also* Constantinople

Canonization, 72, 94
Catacomb Church, 160
Cenobitism, 109, 110, 113
China, 44
Church Fathers, 92, 97, 98

Circle of enthusiasts, 153, 154
Collegium Kioviense. See Kiev: college
Communism, 26, 79-87; end of, 90, 139, 147, 163
Confessio Orthodoxa, 96
Constantinople: dependence on, 9, 38, 52-54, 141; fall of, 16, 56, 57, 95; independence of, 15, 54, 58, 73; patriarch of, 2, 15, 18, 49, 54, 71, 75, 144; schism with, 9; synods in, 58, 96. *See also* Byzantium
Council: of Basel (Countercouncil), 141; of Chalcedon, 93; of Ferrara-Florence, 15, 55, 73; (Russian) Local, 25, 26, 65, 68, 102; Moscow, the Great, 59; Second, of Lyon, 140, 141; Second Vatican, 85, 142, 144
Council on the Russian Orthodox Church Affairs, 30, 67, 84, 86
Culturology, 89

Declaration: of loyalty, 49, 82, 83, 160; of repentance, 28, 81, 82
Dekabrists, 100
De-Stalinization, 31, 85
Disarmament, 31
Dissenters, religious, 159-63
Dnepr river, 36, 111
Double faith, 8, 39, 94
Dukhobors, 158, 159